Society of Risk-Takers

Living Life on the Edge

Contemporary Social Issues

George Ritzer, *Series Editor*

Contemporary Social Issues

Series Editor: George Ritzer, *University of Maryland*

Society of Risk-Takers

Living Life on the Edge

William C. Cockerham

University of Alabama at Birmingham

Worth Publishers

Society of Risk-Takers

Acquisitions Editor: Erik Gilg
Executive Marketing Manager: John Britch
Project Editor: Eve Conte
Art Director: Babs Reingold
Cover Design and Photo Research: Lyndall Culbertson
Text Designer: Lissi Sigillo
Production Manager: Barbara Ann Seixas
Composition: Matrix Publishing Services
Printing and Binding: R.R. Donnelley
Cover Credit: Daniel Arsenault/Getty Images

Library of Congress Control Number 2005930647

ISBN: 0-7167-5542-4 (EAN: 9780716755425)

© 2006 by Worth Publishers

Printed in the United States of America

First printing 2005

Worth Publishers
41 Madison Avenue
New York, NY 10010
www.worthpublishers.com

To Cynthia—Whose only risk taking was marrying me.

About the Author

William C. Cockerham holds a Ph.D. from the University of California, Berkeley. He is Distinguished Professor of Sociology, Medicine, and Public Health at the University of Alabama at Birmingham and was the 2004 recipient of the university's Ireland Award for Scholarly Distinction. His recent books include Medical Sociology, 10th edition (2006), The Blackwell Companion to Medical Sociology (2005), and the Sociology of Mental Disorder, 7th edition (2004).

Contents

Foreword

As we move into the twenty-first century, we confront a seemingly endless array of pressing social issues: urban decay, inequality, ecological threats, rampant consumerism, war, AIDS, inadequate health care, national and personal debt, and many more. Although such problems are regularly dealt with in newspapers, magazines, and trade books and on radio and television, such popular treatments have severe limitations. But by examining these issues systematically through the lens of sociology, we can gain greater insight into them and be better able to deal with them. It was to this end that St. Martin's Press created this series on contemporary social issues, and Worth Publishers has chosen to continue it.

Each book in the series casts a new and distinctive light on a familiar social issue, while challenging the conventional view, which may obscure as much as it clarifies. Phenomena that seem disparate and unrelated are shown to have many commonalities and to reflect a major, but often unrecognized, trend within the larger society. Or a systematic comparative investigation demonstrates the existence of social causes or consequences that are overlooked by other types of analysis. In uncovering such realities the books in this series are much more than intellectual exercises; they have powerful practical implications for our lives and for the structure of society.

At another level, this series fills a void in book publishing. There is certainly no shortage of academic titles, but those books tend to be introductory texts for undergraduates or advanced monographs for professional scholars. Missing are broadly accessible, issue-oriented books appropriate for all students (and for general readers). The books in this series occupy that niche somewhere between popular trade books and monographs. Like trade books, they deal with important and interesting social issues, are well written, and are as jargon free as possible. However, they are more rigorous than trade books in meeting academic standards for writing and research. Although they are not textbooks, they often explore topics covered in basic textbooks and therefore are easily integrated into the curriculum of sociology and other disciplines.

Each of the books in the "Contemporary Social Issues" series is a new and distinctive piece of work. I believe that students, serious general readers, and professors will all find the books to be informative, interesting, thought provoking, and exciting. Among the topics to be covered in forthcoming additions to the series are the declining wealth and increasing indebtedness of the middle class and the speculative nature of American financial markets.

—*George Ritzer*

Preface

The reader might think that the author of this book is a chain-smoking, drug-addicted, alcoholic bungee jumper with a sexually transmitted disease or two. Actually, I am none of these things. But I must admit that in writing this book, I sometimes thought some first-hand experience would be useful in making a particular point or describing a specific situation. However, I probably should interject that I have engaged in some forms of risk-taking and so am not a complete novice. My risk-taking moments usually happened when as a young man I served in the Army Airborne and Special Forces. More than once during this time it was necessary for me to engage in edgework, actions that brought me to the boundary between potential harm and safety. Sometimes this was scary and other times it was great fun. So even though I never tried to smoke myself to death, do not take drugs, or show any signs of becoming an alcoholic, I am confident that I know what risk taking involves and can explain it in sociological terms.

To help me understand why people take risks that can damage their health and may even kill them, I relied on the accounts of others in the literature and occasionally in the flesh. For example, why do people smoke? Being a regular smoker increases the probability of dying from of lung cancer, which seems to be a very unpleasant way to experience the end of one's life, and also shortens it. Logically, then, it would seem a not very intelligent thing to do, yet even intelligent people are (though perhaps increasingly less often) smokers. So the goal of the chapter on smoking, as it was for the other chapters, on sexually transmitted diseases, alcohol, drugs, and extreme sports, was to explain the reasons why people engage in a type of behavior when it is generally acknowledged that the end result can be so harmful. Is the act worth the consequences?

In looking at risk-taking from this perspective, I discovered a couple of key points that I did not find fully represented in the risk-taking literature. First, taking risks is not just a matter of individual personality—although personality is an important contributor. Rather, whether in the form of smoking, sex, or extreme sports, risk taking has its origins in social groups and involves other people. These others are necessary to either initiate or train the novice in the risk-taking activity and/or to serve as a social audience providing support, reassurance, approval, and perhaps even acclaim. Consequently, *risk-taking is a social activity* and as such it has a strong sociological component in terms of class, gender, age, and the like. Second, when it comes to considerations of agency (the capacity to choose) and structure (rules and resources that either empower or constrain), a risk-taking continuum exists from high to low. At the high end are risk-takers like participants in extreme sports who actively seek out risks and have the resources to engage in these daring activities. My first exposure to such people came when I was a kid and went to a local amusement park to ride the roller coaster. At the critical moment, just as the roller coaster reached its greatest height and was on the verge of plunging downward, some of my friends would stand up and raise both hands in the air to maximize the thrill by adding the danger of falling out of the carriage. Fortunately, no one ever did.

Other risk-takers, in contrast, are at the lower end of the risk-response continuum. These are passive risk-takers who take risks because the structure of their social life leaves them with little or no choice. An example comes from an experience I had in an East African town when I was in the Army. The town was full of commercial truck drivers resting before resuming their run and prostitutes who made their living providing sex to the drivers. One day some of the men I was with began a conversation with a prostitute outside a hotel, asking her why she performed this kind of work given the near- certainty she would be infected by HIV/AIDS. She replied that there were few jobs for women in Africa outside the home and she had to work to support herself. Without an income, she could not survive. Once more, we reminded her of the likelihood that she would get AIDS. "I know that," she said simply, "but I have to live."

It is the intent of this book to try to understand the varieties of harmful risks and the reasons people make such choices. Hopefully, the risk-response model proposed in these pages and the evidence that supports it, will advance our understanding of the social aspects of risk taking.

—*William C. Cockerham*
Birmingham, Alabama

Acknowledgements

Risk-taking has been a fascinating topic to explore, and I would like to thank George Ritzer who suggested I contribute a book on it to the series on social issues that he edits for Worth Publishers. Not only did George provide important insights on a variety of issues, he was available for support throughout this project. Additionally, I owe a debt of gratitude to Erik Gilg, my editor at Worth, for his sound advice and outstanding competence. It has been a pleasure to work with him. I would also like to acknowledge the excellent editing of the manuscript provided by Eve Conte and her associates. They did one of the best jobs of copy editing I have ever experienced in the several books I have authored. Finally, I would like to thank Ferris Ritchey, Chair of the Sociology Department of the University of Alabama at Birmingham, for providing an environment for scholarship.

The Social Nature of Risk

Daily life can be a risky business. Simply crossing a street in traffic, driving through a red light, smoking cigarettes, and eating high-fat foods can be hazardous to one's health. Some people avoid taking such risks, yet others do these things even though they are aware of the potential harm. Why? What causes someone to be a risk-taker? The purpose of this book is to look at this question from a sociological perspective and provide some answers regarding risky behaviors like smoking and sky diving that can kill the person who risks doing them. This book then is not about people who risk their money by gambling, but it is about people who risk their health and their lives by gambling with them.

The advantage of using a sociological viewpoint to study risk is that human behavior, including risk behavior, is inherently social. That is, although people can and do act alone, their behavior usually occurs either in concert with that of other people or in social settings where other people or the setting itself influences the action that goes on there. Even if we see ourselves as rational individuals in control of our own actions, in reality, social processes both inside and outside our everyday world influence our behavior and guide us in particular directions. We do not have to follow these directions, but we customarily do what we deem practical in the context of the circumstance we find ourselves in. Acting practically usually means conforming to what others are doing in the same setting. Consequently, taking risks is not just something individuals typically decide to do independently of others or of the settings where they find themselves. Other people and social groups are usually involved because risk-takers look to them for motivation as well as seek approval, recognition, respect, support, or even shock in response to their actions. To take a risk is a social act; so sociological perspectives help us understand the dynamics of that act.

In economics and business, we can calculate risks with respect to costs, benefits, and probabilities for success. In these domains, risks can be attractive, if the potential for loss is slight while the potential for gain is high as measured by increasing profits or establishing a stronger position in the marketplace. Or risks can have a high probability of leading to disaster if one or more things goes wrong. Sometimes the greater the risk, the greater the benefits and as well the greater the possible loss. The risk-taker must decide if taking the risk is worth the harm that will occur should the action be unsuccessful or worth the benefit if it turns out well.

Although outcomes can be either positive or negative, risks themselves are generally regarded as negative. As Australian sociologist Deborah Lupton observes, over the course of the twentieth century, distinctions in everyday language between good and bad risks tended to fade.[1] For most people, the term *risk* came to mean more or less exclusively danger, threat, or harm. There was no such thing as a good risk, because risks in themselves signified something potentially bad. According to Mary Douglas, "the word *risk* now means danger; *high risk* means a lot of danger."[2]

In this book, *risk* is viewed as a situation or action involving danger for the risk-taker and possibly for others who have risks imposed on them by someone else. The focus will be on why people pursue certain risky behaviors that may adversely affect their health and possibly even lead to their death. These behaviors include risks involving HIV/AIDS and sexually-transmitted diseases, alcohol abuse, drug abuse, smoking, and extreme sports. A common thread linking them is that, as noted, taking risks is not simply a random act of individuals, it is embedded in certain social situations and is, moreover, widespread in contemporary society.

Risk and Society

Some behavioral science literature suggests that certain people have personalities predisposing them to take risks, while the personalities of other people cause them to shy away from risky situations. Probably most people would say that their life experiences have shown that both these notions are true. But, as Stephen Lyng points out, the main shortcoming of risk-prone personality theories is that they do not explain what causes the personality predisposition toward risk to exist in the first place.[3] Some people, for example, may have a predisposition toward risk taking because it provides them with excitement, but why they are predisposed toward wanting or needing excitement is not known. Research seeking to identify the personality types attracted to risk taking is still inconclusive, although some people have personalities that mark them as risk-takers.

Another potential explanation for why some people are risk-takers is that they have an intrinsic psychological need for arousal or stimulation. Such individuals are usually easily bored and unhappy with day-to-day routines. They seem to crave the stimulation that comes with risk taking. Yet Lyng suggests that these kinds of explanations typically fail to account for the influence of the broader social conditions and the settings within which risk taking occurs. Consequently, the social context in which people feel a need for arousal satisfied by taking risks is left unspecified.

Despite such problems, theories pertaining to personality and intrinsic motivations are important because they help us to understand why various psychological factors like a desire for thrills are involved in risk taking. But Lyng is correct in noting that such theories often do not consider the social context that both activate these psychological factors and provide the situational background for their expression. It is necessary to take into account social conditions and structures to formulate complete explanations. A considerable body of sociological literature details the influence of social structures on individual behavior.[4] Social structures constrain people in many ways, including by establishing norms for behavior. But social structures also empower people to act in certain ways. As the late French sociologist Pierre Bourdieu observed, individual dispositions toward acting in particular ways tend to be compatible with the guidelines set by society; therefore, usual and practical forms of behavior—not unpredictable novelty—typically prevail.[5]

Social structure is experienced by individuals in three different modes: institutional, relational, and embodied.[6] *Institutional* structure (i.e., institutions, roles) refers to cultural or normative standards of behavior that define how people are supposed to behave in particular situations and form the basis for enduring relationships. *Relational* structure (i.e., status differences, group affiliations, social-class membership) pertains to social relationships and patterns of interconnection and interdependence associated with positions people occupy in society. *Embodied* structure (i.e., language, styles of self-presentation) includes the perceptions and habits by which people produce or reproduce institutional and relational structures, as well as the bodily deportment and nuances of deference and demeanor that express social position. These structural forms illustrate the influence of external social factors like groups, classes, and the wider society on the perceptions of the individual and, as noted, operate to guide behavior in one direction rather than another.

Bourdieu maintains that the tendency of people to act in an orderly, predictable manner is due to the individual's organized system of behavior that he calls a *habitus*.[7] The habitus is a set of durable perceptions about the world formed through upbringing, experience, and the reality of the person's class circumstances. In each of us, our habitus produces enduring dispositions toward action that are more or less routine or habitual, and which become our usual ways of behaving. Although Bourdieu maintains that the habitus does not induce the same response to all situations since it can be creative in responding to old and new circumstances, it nonetheless predisposes the individual to act in ways that are invariably consistent with the socially approved behavioral pathways of the larger social order or some class or group therein.

Bourdieu does not mean by this that people act in a mechanical, robotic, and unthinking fashion as dictated by social structure via the habitus; rather, he means that we generally take structural influences into account when making decisions about how to behave. It is through the habitus that awareness of society enters into the person's thinking and provides him or her with specifications about how to act. The process of thought by which individual actors critically evaluate and choose courses of action is known as agency. Structure either empowers agency or constrains it by limiting choices to what is possible. As Polish sociologist Zygmunt Bauman observes, individual choices in all circumstances are confined by two sets of constraints: (1) choosing from among what is available, and (2) social rules or codes informing the individual of the rank order and appropriateness of preferences.[8] While agency theorists maintain that agency will never be completely determined by structure, it is also clear "there is no hypothetical moment in which agency actually gets 'free' of structure; it is not, in other words, some pure [form of] transcendental free will."[9] If agency refers to the capacity to choose behavior, structure pertains to regularities in social interaction and social relationships that offer a script for behavioral choices.

The effects of structure on risk behavior are, however, not known. Structure may repress tendencies toward risk taking, since structural influences tend to produce stable, orderly behavior. But in some circumstances, structure may actually induce risky behavior in certain people, groups, and classes. A key factor here may be whether the risk is controllable and not terribly frightening, compared to risks that are not controllable and very frightening. The latter are the most risky of all and may involve agency overruling structure. Nevertheless, both agency and structure are so closely linked and are the necessary components of any form of behavior that each likely plays some role in any risk-taking scenario. Theories explaining risk taking therefore need to incorporate considerations of societal factors (structure) into accounts of individual choices (agency) to confront risks. It is the intention of this book to examine the social factors that promote risk. Before discussing specific types of risk involved in sexually-transmitted diseases, alcohol abuse, and the like, the remainder of this chapter will look at risk perspectives that currently influence the research of sociologists. Included are the work of Mary Douglas, Ulrich Beck, Anthony Giddens, Michel Foucault, and Stephen Lyng.

Douglas: Risk and Culture

British cultural anthropologist Mary Douglas sought to explain why some dangers in society are regarded as more risky than others.[10] Extremely critical of risk studies in psychology that focused exclusively on the individual, Douglas, believed that the perception of risk is not a private matter. Rather, risks are a cultural phenomenon in that notions of risks and what to do about them are shared with other people in a cultural context. Culture provides a common community orientation toward risks by helping us define them, calculate their degree of danger, and ascertain their probable consequences. Responses to risk are therefore much more than simply the cognitive or psychological reactions of individuals. Group and social perceptions about risks are determining factors in risk-taking ventures as well. As Douglas and her colleague Aaron Wildavsky suggest, risk is a *collective* [or socially constructed] concept.[11]

Douglas and Wildavsky developed a risk-response model that depicts four types of people who differ in the way they cope with risk. The four groups are: (1) *hierarchists*, who respect authority, conform closely to group norms and expectations concerning risk, and trust established organizations to deal with them; (2) *egalitarians*, who strongly identify with their group, blame outsiders for risky situations, support social equality, and believe in taking a participatory approach (organized community action) toward risk; (3) *individualists*, who are individualistic and entrepreneurial, distrust organizations, sometimes see risks as opportunities, and believe in handling risks themselves; and (4) *fatalists*, who lack strong group ties, tend to think they have little control over risk, and trust risky outcomes to fate or luck.

Douglas illustrates the applicability of the model with an example of HIV/AIDS risk in a city. She notes how hierarchists (the dominant group) would typically use the city's government and official organizations to deal with the threat. Egalitarians (dissenting minority groups and AIDS activists) would distrust the city and organize their own groups to ensure that the city was not being discriminatory in its allocation of resources. Individualists, in turn, would leave it up to individuals while fatalists would leave it to fate or luck to cope with the risk.[12]

Although this model has been criticized for being too rigid and perhaps too general in its assignment of people to different categories, Douglas's approach to the study of risk has been influential not only in anthropology, but also sociology. Considered in its entirety, her model counters the exclusive focus in risk research on individuals and their personalities, by describing the relevance of culture and the larger social order for risk perceptions and responses.[13]

Beck: The Risk Society

The English language version of German sociologist Ulrich Beck's book, *The Risk Society: Towards a New Modernity*, appeared in 1992 and became a major statement about the nature of risk in contemporary society.[14] Beck maintained that the industrial age was ending. and with its demise, risks were taking on a different character. He states: *"Just as modernization dissolved the structure of feudal society in the nineteenth century and produced the industrial society, modernization is dissolving industrial society and another modernity is coming into being."*[15]

Some scholars refer to this other modernity as "high" or "post-modernity," but Beck simply calls it a "second modernity." What we need to realize, Beck insists, is that modernization ages and an important facet of this ongoing development is the emergence of the risk society. The risk society describes an era in which the individual, social, political, and economic risks created by the momentum of innovation increasingly elude the control and protective institutions of industrial society.[16] Beck defines risks *"as a systematic way of dealing with hazards and insecurities induced by modernization itself."*[17] The very technologies that have produced the industrial society are giving birth to the risk society.

For example, automobiles are responsible for the greatest number of adolescent deaths. People in the general population are harmed as well. Yet larger and faster death-dealing automobiles continue to be produced, and people are encouraged through advertising to acquire them. In this case, an industry intrinsic to the process of modernization—the automobile industry—is producing life-threatening risks and does so with very few limitations. Similar examples may be found in the nuclear and chemical industries whose products are essential to modern societies, but whose wastes contaminate the environment.

Beck uses the term *reflexive modernization* to describe the stages of modernization associated with the risk society. First, is the *reflex stage*, in which the risks produced by modernization during the transition from the industrial to the risk society are subject to little or no public or political debate. Second, is the *reflection stage*, in which society comes to see itself as a risk society and begins to realize the danger, while initiating steps to cope with it. This critical reflection on the harm posed by modernity is, in Beck's view, the difference between an industrial society and a risk society. Awareness of the risks associated with modernization promotes the demise of the industrial era with its unchecked risky technology and methods of exploiting the natural environment.

Beck observes that some risks—like unemployment, slum housing, greater violence and crime, and a lack of personal security—are more commonly experienced by the poor. But the affluent in a risk society also face hazards that cannot be easily escaped, such as air, water, and soil pollution that transcend social and national boundaries. The accidental release of radiation into the air in 1986 by the Chernobyl nuclear power plant in Ukraine in the former Soviet Union, for example, affected both rich and poor, with westerly winds spreading the radiation as far as Sweden. Beck comments that today a *boomerang effect* ensures that locating a hazardous industry in a particular country or part of town will not necessarily protect the wealthy or others living elsewhere. Everyone is at risk in the risk society.

Beck suggests that the public belief in the message of the Enlightenment that science is an invariably positive force in human progress is shattered in the risk society, with science itself bringing about unintentional threats to well-being through its industrial practices. The risk society is not an option, explains Beck, because it "arises through the automatic operations of autonomous modernization processes, which are blind and deaf to consequences and danger."[18] The result, he maintains, is our world today where we are faced with at least three major threats that are global in their impact. First, is the ecological destruction and technological danger associated with the disregard for the environment that can accompany the production of wealth. The second and third risks are those of poverty and the use of weapons of mass destruction. Both these risks, however, can also be linked to the environment, as pollution "follows" the poor, thereby intensifying their disadvantages, while a major cause of armed conflict is control over vitally necessary resources like oil. Thus, the world we live in is a risky place, and many of its risks are beyond the control of any one individual. People are therefore left to seek out and construct their own certainties. That is, they are required to develop their own protective measures against risks because they cannot always depend on the government and certainly not on business corporations to look out for their welfare. Beck does not confront the entire range of risks that individuals may face. But he alerts us to the role of modernization in making life a more risky proposition, especially with respect to environmental pollution. His ideas, about the way large corporations make the world a risky place to live even though their products are intended to improve life, were very attractive to university students in the 1980s, and he remains a popular figure in sociology.

Giddens: Runaway World

British sociologist Anthony Giddens views modernity as a huge juggernaut producing a "runaway world" overwhelming tradition with its changes.[19] Among these changes is a proliferation of risks. Giddens finds that, apart from some marginal abstractions, there was no well-defined concept of risk during the Middle Ages. The idea of risk seems to have first gained popularity in the sixteenth and seventeenth centuries when European explorers set off for the unknown lands and uncharted waters of the New World. For example, in Portuguese, one root meaning of risk is "to dare." Hence, to take a risk meant taking a dare or chance at doing something dangerous whose outcome is uncertain and potentially harmful. Later, explains Giddens, notions of risk were applied to banking and investment and came to signify situations of uncertainty involving financial outcomes. Modern capitalism evolved by accepting risk as a continuous process, with the potential for profits and losses in the future guiding transactions in the present. The rise of the insurance industry was, in fact, stimulated by people willing to pay to protect themselves and their property from hazards associated with risks. The first forms of insurance, not surprisingly, began with seafaring in the sixteenth century, since going to sea was a risky business because of the high potential for ships and cargoes being lost to foul weather or pirates. Owners wanted their property insured in case of loss, since such losses could ruin their business.

Giddens argues that while the idea of risk has always been an aspect of modernity, the current historical period is witness to a new form of it. We now are exposed to what he calls manufactured risks which he defines as risks created by the impact of our knowledge on the world. Global warming is an example of a manufactured risk in that it is caused by the adverse effects of chemical gases and fumes released into the air by motor vehicles and industrial plants, both of which destroy the ozone. This effect is not brought about by nature, but results from products developed through the use of scientific knowledge. "At a certain point," concludes Giddens, "however—very recently in historical terms—we started worrying less about what nature can do to us, and more about what we have done to nature."[20]

Giddens's position is that the current phase of modernity is not necessarily more dangerous or risky, because there have often been high-risk periods in the past. What is different is that new risks caused by the unintended consequences of modernization like global ecological risk and nuclear proliferation have emerged. To contend with these kind of risks, the public is forced to rely on scientists and governments. But scientists often disagree, and governments can be slow to respond or be stymied by politics when various interest groups maneuver to influence their policies. Sometimes governments may cover up the true extent of a risk not to alarm the general population or disrupt economic activities.

This was the case in China in 2002, when the initial outbreak of the severe acute respiratory syndrome (SARS) threatened to become a global pandemic. At first, the Chinese government denied that a serious and previously unknown infectious disease was spreading in Quangdong Province. A businessman was the first to become sick there, and he infected enough doctors and nurses to fill a hospital ward. In February 2003, a Chinese doctor who had treated SARS patients in Quangdong Province traveled to Hong Kong for a wedding. He felt ill after he arrived. The doctor had SARS and subsequently died but not before infecting other people at his hotel. One of the infected was a Chinese-American businessman who went on to travel to Hanoi in Vietnam and died but not before spreading the disease there; another was a Chinese-Canadian grandmother who carried SARS home to Toronto, where she too died after spreading the infection.

An Italian physician, Carlo Urbani, doing medical research in Vietnam was asked to consult on the case in Hanoi. He determined that the patient had a previously unknown and highly infectious disease. Dr. Urbani initiated anti-infection procedures in the local hospital that helped contain the disease, convinced Vietnamese health officials they had an epidemic in their midst, and notified the World Health Organization. WHO issued an alert and countries around the world started screening travelers. The Chinese Government finally admitted the problem and began to take public measures to halt the infection.

The real hero of this crisis was Dr. Urbani who sounded the first alarm in Hanoi and later died from SARS himself. The Chinese Government subsequently fired the Minister of Health and some other officials who had authority in matters of public health. SARS was eventually contained, but many people became sick, mostly in China, and several hundred died.

Giddens earlier concluded that government policies and scientific findings cannot be accepted at face value. Since governments sometimes cover up problems and scientists may be wrong, governments need to publicly acknowledge risks and strong evidence supporting scientific claims is necessary. But Giddens argues that everyone, not just scientists and governments, needs to be involved in risk management because risks can harm everyone.

Giddens's discussion of risk is similar to that of Beck's, in that both theorists view what Giddens calls manufactured risk as a central concern in contemporary society resulting from modernization.[21] Many risks are indeed produced by modern economies. Both Giddens and Beck recognize, accordingly, that the nature of risk has changed in the present era and that politics have become increasingly important in dealing with risks affecting the public. Both also find that the general public is less likely to rely on the unsupported claims of experts to identify and solve these risks. But Beck differs from Giddens in maintaining that a greater number of risks are being produced today than ever before. In contrast, Giddens suggests that people are far more sensitive to the possibility of risk in the present era and more alert to its potential than in the past—so it just seems like there is more risk. Nevertheless, he too finds that the concept of risk has great relevance for our time and constitutes a basic characteristic of the world we live in.

Foucault: Governmentality

The concept of risk was not a major topic for the late French theorist Michel Foucault, yet his ideas have been used by a few scholars to theorize about the role of government in containing threats to society. *Governmentality* is a term coined by Foucault to refer to efforts of social regulation and governmental control that emerged in sixteenth-century Europe.[22] As the feudal social system began to break down, administrative bureaucracies evolved to manage the affairs of government. These bureaucracies were organized on the basis of formal rules and regulations that generally stipulated appropriate forms of conduct for the citizenry, such as paying taxes and fees. By the eighteenth century, the concept of governmentality, in Foucault's view, was well established. The governments of the modern European states of the time saw their citizens as populations that had to be controlled and protected to ensure social stability, the political status quo, and economic productivity. Implied in this arrangement is the notion that governments have the duty to intervene when their welfare and that of their citizens are threatened with risk. Controlling risk thus became a form of regulatory power by governments on their own behalf by which populations were monitored, managed, and analyzed. As part of this effort, governments began to collect large amounts of data on income, crime, fertility, life expectancy, mortality, and other areas relevant to their own interests.

Foucault provided social histories of the ways in which such knowledge was used by trained professions and institutions to monitor and manage populations on behalf of governments. For example, the justice system controlled criminals and medicine managed the sick. Expert knowledge about particular areas of social life thus became a source of power, since it was used to control people. Knowledge and power were depicted by Foucault as so closely connected that an extension of one meant a simultaneous expansion of the other. In his studies of prisons and medical clinics, he often used the singular term *knowledge/power* to express this unity. In reviewing the history of medicine, for example, Foucault identified two distinct trends. He referred to one as "medicine of the species" (the classification, diagnosis, and treatment of disease) and the other as "medicine of social spaces" (the prevention of disease).[23] Medicine of the species defined the human body as an object of study subject to medical intervention and control, while medicine of social spaces made the public's health subject to medical and civil regulation. Public health authorities had the mandate to prevent the risk of epidemics and control outbreaks of contagious diseases in the population when they occurred. The merit of Foucault's work for risk taking is that he explains how risks that threaten the social order came to be regarded as eventualities that governments were responsible for managing.

Lyng: Edgework

Beck, Giddens, and Foucault were concerned with macro- or large-scale risk processes and their management. In contrast, Stephen Lyng focuses on risk at the level of small groups and individuals. Lyng introduces the term *edgework* in sociological research on risk taking to describe voluntary participation in dangerous occupations or leisure-time activities.[24] Edgework refers to circumstances in which the skilled performance of a dangerous activity is the focus for the individual as well as for others who witness the action. Edgework essentially means skirting the edge between safety and danger. It requires of the risk-taking person a high degree of mental toughness not to give in to fear and maintain control over the situation. Losing control would put life and limb at serious risk. To be a success at this is something that its practitioners believe only a few achieve. Such individuals do not consider risk taking to be foolhardy but a confirmation of their own exceptional personal skills that allow them to risk danger without harm.

Activities that constitute edgework have one common feature: they all involve a clear and observable threat to a person's physical or mental well-being or sense of an ordered existence.[25] "The archetypical edgework experience," states Lyng, "is one in which the individual's failure to meet the challenge at hand will result in death or, at the very least, debilitating injury."[26] High-risk sports like sky diving, hang gliding, rock climbing, motorcycle or car racing, and downhill ski racing are examples of edgework, as are dangerous occupations like combat soldiering, police work, fire fighting, test piloting, and stunt work in movies. Lyng comments:

> People who devote leisure time to such activities as home improvement and fishing do so in part because these activities allow for the development and use of various skills. But edgeworkers claim to possess a special ability, one that transcends activity-specific skills, such as those needed for driving a car, riding a motorcycle, and flying an airplane or one's body in free-fall. This unique skill, which applies to all types of edgework, is the ability to maintain control over a situation that verges on complete chaos, a situation most people would regard as entirely uncontrollable. The more specific aptitudes required for this type of competence involve the ability to avoid being paralyzed by fear and the capacity to focus one's attention and actions on what is most crucial for survival. Thus, most edgeworkers regard this general skill as essentially cognitive in nature, and they often refer to it as a special form of "mental toughness.[27]

What someone gains from his or her successful performance is a sense of exhilaration and omnipotence. The person feels capable of dealing with threatening situations, and these feelings contribute to a self-definition of being elite for both the individual and his or her group of fellow edgeworkers. People attracted to edgework in their leisure time, according to Lyng, frequently have full-time employment that by being routine, lacks the challenges that would satisfy their desire to put themselves at risk and succeed at it. They are usually males since males are more likely than females to develop an orientation through socialization that leads them to believe that they can control their environment.

However, Lyng also finds that edgeworkers are not typically interested in mere thrill seeking or gambling because they dislike being in threatening circumstances they cannot control or placing themselves in the control of others—like operators at amusement park rides—whose competence is unknown. Thus, they like do not like to leave their well-being to others or to the whims of fate. What edgeworkers seek is a chance to use their *skill* in dealing with a challenge, not turning their fate over to someone else or the roll of the dice. Their own personal competence is what they want to put at risk, so they can draw on their own performance to construct an image of themselves as members of an elite.

Summary

The views presented in this section represent important contemporary sociological approaches toward explaining risk. Each of these perspectives offers insight, but none fully explain the risk experience. Douglas indicates that defining and taking risks is not just a matter of personal psychology in which an individual decides to do something risky. Rather, risks are perceived, acted out, and interpreted in a particular cultural and social context. Beck and Giddens are both concerned with the technological risks that accompany modernity and note how scientific progress often produces unintended risks that harm the environment and people's lives. The challenge is to be aware of these risks and mobilize public resources to contain them. Foucault's work helps us understand how governments and experts are increasingly called on to manage risks for the populations they administer. But Foucault relies primarily on abstract discourses about risk management and does not consider how people actually respond to risk situations.

Lyng introduces the notion of edgework which describes why certain individuals volunteer to walk the edge between safety and danger to demonstrate their personal competence. He offers some background on the characteristics of edgeworkers regarding gender and occupation, but his portrayal of such individuals shows that a limited number of people are involved and the risks they take are just those they feel they can control—regardless of the outcome. Thus, his ideas apply only to a few risk-takers.

The theoretical approaches of Douglas, Beck, Giddens, and Foucault are, in contrast, obviously meant to apply to more general risk situations where much larger numbers of people or populations are involved either voluntarily or involuntarily. The problem with these perspectives is not so much with what they say, but what they do not say. Basic questions about the social characteristics of people most likely to take risks and the social situations where they are influenced to engage in risk taking have yet to be fully articulated. Each of these theorists addresses only limited aspects of risk situations. Obviously, additional work is necessary to round out existing perspectives or construct new and more comprehensive theories of risk taking. Despite these problems, each of these theories does offer insight into selected features of risk taking and helps to create a foundation for future research.

Risk Taking: Age and Gender

One general feature of risk taking that seems universal is the structural role of age and gender. Lupton notes that risk taking is a gendered performance.[28] What she means is that males are significantly more likely to engage in risk taking than females, especially young males, those in their teens and twenties. Getting drunk, taking drugs, having sex at an early age, speeding in cars, engaging in petty theft, committing vandalism, standing up in roller-coasters, and like behaviors are much more typical of young males than females or older males. Young males do such things, Lupton suggests, because it adds thrills to their life, tests their courage, and also because they believe it proves their masculinity and prowess. Lupton bases her assessment on an extensive review of the research literature showing that girls are much more likely than boys to avoid taking risks that cause accidents, as well as better at ensuring the safety of others, accepting adult authority, not courting danger or proving bravery in front of others.

Another example of young males constituting the preponderance of people taking risks is seen in crime statistics. Age is a consistent predictor of criminal activity. FBI statistics show year after year that the majority of people (70 percent) arrested for major crimes in the United States are under the age of 29 years and more than half are between the ages of 15 and 24 years.[29] Those persons who begin criminal activities early in life are more likely to be adult offenders as well.

Comparisons of the involvement of men and women in criminal activities also show a consistent pattern. Members of both sexes commit all types of crimes, but men commit disproportionately more of them. On an annual basis, about 85 percent of all people arrested for major crimes are male.[30] Kathleen Harris and her colleagues found in a nationwide study that males constituted the majority of adolescents who felt they had "nothing to lose" by engaging in risky behavior because they did not see a good future awaiting them.[31] Although somewhat more young males than young females were likely to engage in early sexual intercourse, young males were considerably more likely to sell drugs and use weapons. Still, while it can be claimed that overall risk-takers are more common among males than females, it is important to note that some females do take risks and that females also may be victimized by male risk-takers. So females are not absent from the risk situation.

Health Lifestyles and Risk Taking

When people routinely take risks over a period of time, their risk-taking behavior becomes part of their lifestyle. When the risks are health related, then obviously they are part of that person's health lifestyle. *Health lifestyles* are collective patterns of health-related behavior based on choices from options available to people according to their life chances.[32] This definition is based on German sociologist Max Weber's seminal work on lifestyles.[33] Weber (1864–1920) suggested that a person's life choices and life chances interact with one another in a dialectical manner, with choices constrained or enabled by chances and likely to be consistent with the capability to realize them. Life choices are the choices that people have in their selection of lifestyles; life chances are the probabilities of realizing those choices.

British sociologist Ralf Dahrendorf observes that while Weber is vague about what he means by life chances, the best interpretation is that they are "the crystallized probability of finding satisfaction for interests, wants and needs, thus the probability of the occurrence of events which bring about satisfaction."[34] The probability of acquiring satisfaction is anchored in structural conditions that are largely economic—involving income, property, the opportunity for profit, and the like—but Dahrendorf suggests that the concept of life chances also includes rights, norms, and social relationships (the probability that others will respond in a certain manner). Dahrendorf points out that Weber does not consider life chances to be a matter of pure chance; rather, they are the chances people have in life because of their social situation. Weber's overall thesis is that life chances are socially determined and social structure is an arrangement of life chances. Hence, lifestyles are not random behaviors unrelated to structure but typically are deliberate choices influenced by life chances.

Consequently, Dahrendorf and his colleagues assert that Weber's most important contribution to conceptualizing lifestyles in sociological terms is to identify the dialectical relationship between choice and chance in lifestyle determination.[35] Choices and chances interact to determine a distinctive lifestyle for individuals and groups. The identification of life chances as the opposite of life choices in Weber's lifestyle dialectic provides the key to helping us understand the manner in which lifestyles are operationalized in the real world. It can be said that individuals have a range of freedom, but not complete freedom in choosing a lifestyle because of the social constraints that apply to their situation in life. Lifestyle constraints are largely, but not entirely, socioeconomic in origin. Those with the desire and the means may choose more fully; those lacking these in some way cannot choose so easily and may find their lifestyle determined more by circumstances than by choice.

When it comes to health lifestyles, the behaviors that are generated from the interplay of choices and chances can have either positive or negative consequences on body and mind, but nonetheless produce an overall pattern of health practices. Health lifestyles include contact with medical professionals for checkups and preventive care, but the majority of health activities occur outside health-care delivery systems. These activities typically include choices and practices that range from brushing one's teeth and using automobile seatbelts to relaxing at health spas. For most people, health lifestyles involve decisions about food, exercise, smoking, and alcohol use, along with safe sex, relaxation, personal hygiene, risk of accidents, coping with stress, and having physical checkups.

Bourdieu finds lifestyles to be generally oriented toward practical outcomes mediated by the habitus.[36] The habitus, as described earlier in this chapter, is an individual's organized repertoire of perceptions that guide and evaluate behavioral choices and options. It is a mindset that produces a relatively enduring collection of dispositions to act in particular ways. These dispositions typically reflect the normative structure of the larger society and generate stable and consistent lifestyle practices. Individuals, as discussed, are neither totally free, nor the mere bearers of external social structures in this arrangement. They incorporate a practical sense of what is possible or impossible to achieve in their habitus. The habitus then produces dispositions channeling behavior in particular directions rather than alternative behaviors that might be chosen. People typically take these pathways, because it is what they are used to doing and consistent with the social and cultural context of their lives.

The focus of this book, however, is on negative health lifestyle practices that involve risk-taking behavior. For some people, the pathways that their habitus directs them down place their health in jeopardy, by causing them to risk death or injury as a result of their choices. Why would this occur if the habitus is oriented toward stable and practical dispositions that typically reflect social norms? One answer is that normative behavior is relative. Norms that promote risk avoidance for some might not be normative for others who value risk and whose norms put them at risk. Another answer lies in the intersection of agency (choices) and structure (life chances) in the lives of people. For example, a person might not choose to be subject to a risky situation (like contracting HIV), but have little or no choice in the matter because of social-structural conditions that render him or her powerless to do otherwise. This could occur when a woman in a highly dependent status has sexual relations with a more powerful man who refuses to use condoms. To illustrate this type of situation, we will examine a model of risk-taking behavior in the next section.

A Model of Risk-Taking Behavior

Figure 1-1 presents a model of risk-taking behavior that provides the framework for discussing the different types of risks discussed in this book. Figure 1-1 shows agency and structure flanking risk responses, with each existing as a continuum ranging from low to high. When agency is low and structure is constraining, people have low control over their risk responses. Therefore, people at the lowest end of the risk-response continuum can be depicted as in passive denial. Constrained by structural conditions and with a low capacity for agency, they are passive in responding to risk because they believe they cannot do anything about it. As far as they are concerned, fate or luck will decide the outcome. In addition, as the discussion to follow in this book illustrates, a typical coping strategy for members of this group is denial. They deny the risk exists or deny that they will be the ones to be harmed. The example in Figure 1-1 is that of the powerless HIV recipient who was infected by someone who refused to use protection.

Higher up on the risk-response continuum are persons in a passive acceptance mode. They have a somewhat greater capacity for agency and are not as constrained by structure. They could take action to abort the risk, but do not. The example of passive acceptance in Figure 1-1 is that of the dedicated smoker. This is a person who knows his or her health is harmed

Figure 1-1

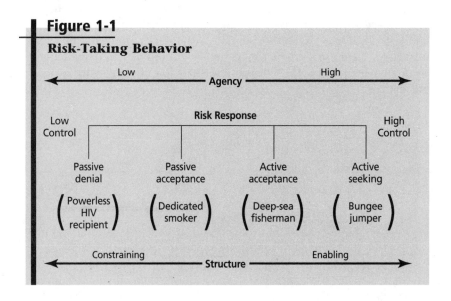

Risk-Taking Behavior

by smoking and life cut short because of it, yet accepts the risk and continues to smoke. The next highest form of risk response is active acceptance. The example is the deep-sea fisherman. Deep-sea fishing is considered by life insurance companies to be the most dangerous civilian occupation. But deep-sea fishermen actively accept the risks because it goes with the job. When storms arise at sea, they can exercise their agency to cope with the situation and are enabled by the structure of their job to work safely in sea-worthy crafts with emergency equipment and have emergency services on call. Nevertheless, a boat sometimes goes down with its crew in stormy weather in Alaskan waters or in the North Atlantic. Being a police officer or combat infantryman in wartime can also be especially dangerous.

At the highest end of the risk-response continuum in Figure 1-1 is the active-seeking mode. This group includes those with a high-agency capacity and high-enabling structure that allow them to actively seek risks. The example is the bungee jumper. The bungee jumper must choose to jump and have the structural resources, such as time and money, to pursue the sport. Persons in this category are the edgeworkers described by Lyng. They skirt the edge between safety and danger and do their utmost to control a high-risk situation to demonstrate their skill and competence. They are the ultimate risk-takers.

In subsequent chapters, we will apply this model of risk-taking behavior to health-threatening forms of risk. First, we will examine risk taking in relation to sexually-transmitted diseases and HIV/AIDS (Chapter 2), followed by an analysis of risk taking associated with alcohol (Chapter 3), illicit drugs (Chapter 4), smoking (Chapter 5), and extreme sports (Chapter 6). The final chapter (Chapter 7) will provide an overall analysis of why people risk their health and their lives by engaging in these practices.

Notes

1. Deborah Lupton. 1999. "Introduction: Risk and Sociocultural Theory." In Deborah Lupton (ed.), *Risk and Sociocultural Theory: New Directions and Perspectives*. Cambridge, UK: Cambridge University Press, pp. 1–11.
2. Mary Douglas. 1992. *Risk and Blame: Essays in Cultural Theory*. London: Routledge, p. 24.

3. Stephen Lyng. 1990. "Edgework: A Social Psychological Analysis of Voluntary Risk Taking." *American Journal of Sociology*, 95: 853.
4. William H. Sewell. 1992. "A Theory of Structure: Duality, Agency, and Transformation." *American Journal of Sociology*, 98: 1–29.
5. Pierre Boudieu. 1997. *Pascalian Meditations*. Translated by Richard Nice. Stanford, CA: Stanford University Press.
6. José López and John Scott. 2000. *Social Structure*. Buckingham, UK: Open University Press.
7. Bourdieu. 1977. *Outline of a Theory of Practice*. Translated by Richard Nice. Cambridge, UK: Cambridge University Press. See also Bourdieu, 1984. *Distinction*. Translated by Richard Nice. Cambridge, MA: Harvard University Press and 1990. *The Logic of Practice*. Translated by Richard Nice. Stanford, CA: Stanford University Press.
8. Zygmunt Bauman. 2000. *Liquid Modernity*. Oxford, UK: Polity.
9. Mustafa Emirbayer and Ann Mische. 1998. "What is Agency?" *American Journal of Sociology*, 103: 853.
10. Douglas, *Risk and Blame*.
11. Mary Douglas and Aaron Wildavsky. 1982. *Risk and Culture*. Berkeley, CA: University of California Press.
12. Douglas, *Risk and Blame*.
13. Lupton. 1999. *Risk*. London: Routledge.
14. Ulrich Beck. 1992. *The Risk Society: Towards a New Modernity*. Translated by Mark Ritter. London: Sage.
15. Ibid., p. 10.
16. Ulrich Beck. 1999. *World Risk Society*. Oxford, UK: Polity.
17. Beck, *Risk Society*, p. 21
18. Beck, *World Risk Society*, p. 73.
19. Giddens, Anthony. 2000. *Runaway World*. New York: Routledge.
20. Ibid., p. 44.
21. Lupton, *Risk*, p. 81.
22. Michel Foucault. 1991. "Governmentality." In G. Burchell, C. Gordon, and P. Miller (eds.), *The Foucault Effect: Studies in Governmentality*. Hernel Hempstead, UK: Wheatsheaf, pp. 87–104.
23. Michel Foucault. 1973. *The Birth of the Clinic*. London: Tavistock.
24. Lyng, pp. 851–886.
25. Ibid., p. 857.
26. Ibid.
27. Ibid., p. 859.
28. Lupton.
29. FBI. 2002. *Crime in the United States, Uniform Crime Reports—2002*. Washington, D.C.: U.S. Government Printing Office.
30. Ibid.

31. Kathleen Mullan Harris, Greg J. Duncan, and Johanne Boisjoly. 2002. "Evaluating the Role of 'Nothing to Lose' Attitudes on Risky Behavior in Adolescence." *Social Forces*, 80: 1005–1039.

32. William C. Cockerham. 2000. "The Sociology of Health Behavior and Health Lifestyles." In Chloe Bird, Peter Conrad, and Allen Fremont (eds.), *Handbook of Medical Sociology*, 5th ed. Upper Saddle River, NJ: Prentice-Hall, pp. 159–171; William C. Cockerham. 2004. *Medical Sociology*, 9th ed. Upper Saddle River, NJ: Prentice-Hall.

33. Max Weber. 1978. *Economy and Society*, 2 vols. Edited by G. Roth and C. Wittich. Berkeley: University of California Press.

34. Ralf Dohrendorf. 1979. *Life Chances*. Chicago: University of Chicago Press, p. 73.

35. William C. Cockerham, Thomas Abel, and Günther Lüschen. 1993. "Max Weber, Formal Rationality, and Health Lifestyles." *Sociological Quarterly*, 34: 413–435.

36. Bourdieu, *Distinction*.

Sexually-Transmitted Diseases and AIDS

Chapter 1 described how social theorists like Ulrich Beck and Anthony Giddens have suggested that modernization is producing major changes in society in the form of contemporary risks. Specifically, the changing society in which we live is producing changing lifestyles that promote a resurgence of risky sexual behaviors. This chapter explores the reasons for this resurgence. The chapter begins with a discussion of the stigma attached to sexual diseases that makes their risk not only biological but social, and it then examines risk behavior associated with the two major types of such diseases: sexually-transmitted diseases (STDS) and HIV/AIDS.

The Spread of Stigmatized Disease

Sexual diseases are diseases of society in the most profound and aberrant sense. Despite exceptions, such as infection through blood transfusions or the sharing of needles in the case of HIV/AIDS, infected adults are typically believed to have placed themselves at risk by violating socially prescribed norms regarding appropriate sexual behavior and partners. As social historian Allan Brandt observes: "Behavior—bad behavior—is seen as the cause of disease."[1] STDS and HIV/AIDS are, in fact, the most socially stigmatizing of all diseases.

According to Erving Goffman, stigma can be defined "as an attribute that is deeply discrediting.[2] Goffman explains that the term *stigma* originated with the ancient Greeks, who used it to refer to marks on the body that symbolized something bad or immoral about the people who had them. Typically, the marks were brands cut or burned into the body to identify the bearer as a criminal, slave, or traitor. When encountering such people, one was expected to avoid them or treat them according to their low-social station. Discrimination was not only socially permissible, but expected. Goffman maintains that stigma in modern society results from three main sources: (1) abominations of the body, such as physical deformities; (2) blemishes of individual character, like mental illness, STDS and AIDS, alcoholism, and suicidal tendencies; and (3) the tribal stigmas of race, religion, and nationality. People with these attributes are not just regarded as different, but different in a negative way and as such frequently subjected to discrimination.

Persons with STDS and AIDS can be characterized as having an abomination of the body, but physical evidence of their disease in its earlier stages is usually not apparent without a blood test. Persons known to have HIV or AIDS, however, are in addition commonly stigmatized as having "a blemish of character" because many believe such diseases are acquired through immoral sexual acts (i.e., outside of wedlock, with disreputable persons, etc.). According to Goffman, stigma represents a rupture between an individual's *virtual* and *actual* social identity that is regarded as failing. A virtual identity is what they *should* have and an actual identity is what they *do* have. The failure to link the two forms of social identity so they are both the same relegates the person to a category of people whose body and perhaps character are tainted.

Kevin Sack reported on the daily lives of HIV-infected American black women in the rural South and found they felt intensely isolated from friends and neighbors.[3] HIV—the human immunodeficiency virus—is the virus that causes the acquired immune deficiency syndrome, known as AIDS. AIDS is a particularly deadly disease that destroys a person's immunity against infection, thereby leaving the individual defenseless against a variety of afflictions like cancer, pneumonia, and a host of viruses. HIV is transmitted through sexual intercourse, intravenous drug use, blood transfusions, or passed to newborn infants by infected mothers. Because of widespread misunderstandings about how HIV is transmitted, the stigma facing the infected women interviewed by Sack was described by him as "often suffocating."

Sack writes:

> Many women are terrified to tell even their families, and they find their only comfort in the monthly meetings of a support group. One woman here, who lives with her son, is convinced he would make her eat off paper plates and would keep her away from her grandchildren if he knew of her illness. [Another woman], who has informed only her family members, said she lost several neighborhood friends after they saw a health department van pull into her driveway to pick her up for a clinic visit.[4]

Even though stigma is imposed on the individual by other people, it can also have a negative effect on a person's self-concept. Stigmatized people often feel devalued and less than normal in public situations. Betsy Fife and Eric Wright investigated the impact of stigma on self-esteem and body image by type of illness, specifically HIV/AIDS and cancer.[5] They found clear evidence that stigma is a central force in the lives of people with both types of illness. Persons with HIV/AIDS reported somewhat stronger feelings of stigma, which is not surprising considering the frequent adverse public characterizations of those infected through homosexuality and intravenous drug use. The more severe the symptoms, the greater the difficulty in concealing the affliction and the stronger the feelings of perceived stigma.

In a truly civil society, one would logically predict a reduction in STDS and AIDS, as self-directed individuals opt for normative and civilizing behaviors that reduce the risk of sexual diseases. According to Norbert Elias, the rise of modern society has been characterized by the general disappearance of physical force in everyday life and an increase in individual self-control and restraint.[6] While historical evidence supports the notion of a civilizing process emerging as early as the tenth century in China (e.g., Confucianism) and the fifteenth century in Europe (e.g., the evolution of table manners and concepts of chivalry, honor, and duty), sexual diseases have obviously not succumbed to this development.

In Europe, other measures instituted during the Middle Ages by society and the church involved the regulation of female sexuality and the patriarchal management of women's bodies. Sex with the wrong person or in the wrong circumstances, as defined by society and the church, was not only immoral, illegal, and a means of spreading sexual disease, it also affected the inheritance of wealth. British sociologist Bryan Turner suggests that an important aspect of this regulation historically was the link between economic production and sexual reproduction.[7] Feudalism and early capitalism required the regulation of women through inheritance systems based on primogeniture (in which the primary heir is the first-born son). The accumulation of family wealth over time was therefore dependent on a line of legitimate male heirs. Thus, female sexuality had to be restricted to that occurring with a husband to whom one was legally wed and whose personal fortunes could be put at risk if his wife had children, especially males, by other men. For the woman, virginity at marriage and fidelity in wedlock were major conditions for economic success. This economic imperative for the regulation of female sexuality was reinforced by the church, which saw such regulation as promoting morality as well as spiritual and social well-being. Although norms for virginity and fidelity were strongest among the upper classes—those most concerned about the preservation of wealth—they evolved into ideal standards of female sexual behavior that persist in a weakened form for society as a whole today.

Throughout most of the twentieth century, rates of sexually-transmitted diseases decreased significantly in the United States and Europe, but the causes for the decline were neither civilizing behaviors nor efforts by men to control promiscuous sexual behavior among marriageable or married females. Rather, this outcome was mainly due to the widespread availability of antibiotics. Even Thomas McKeown, a British epidemiologist widely cited for his observation that society's major infectious diseases had declined before the advent of modern medicine, credited the reduction of syphilis to medical treatment rather than improvements in diet, housing, and sanitation.[8] However, in the 1970s, the situation changed with the dramatic increase in the prevalence of STDS and the introduction of the as yet incurable and deadly AIDS virus into human populations, which reached epidemic proportions in the 1980s. What happened? What caused sexual diseases to spread not just in the United States, but throughout the world?

Laurie Garrett identifies four major factors that explained what was happening: (1) the development of the birth control pill which greatly reduced fears of unwanted pregnancy; (2) an ideology of sexual liberation and greater permissiveness among young urban adults throughout the world; (3) a new pattern of employment in developing nations in which young males migrate to the cities for jobs and return to their villages on weekends to spend time with their spouses and families, thereby spreading sexual diseases acquired in urban areas to the countryside; and (4), perhaps most importantly, the availability of multiple sexual partners on an unprecedented scale.[9] According to Garrett, homosexual men in Europe and North America and young heterosexuals in developing countries, especially Africa, took greatest advantage of the new sexual climate. She explains:

> With over five billion people on the planet, an ever-increasing percentage of whom were urban residents; with air travel and mass transits available to allow people from all over the world to go to cities of their choice; with mass youth movements at their zenith, advocating, among other things, sexual freedom; with a feminist spirit alive in much of the industrialized world, promoting female sexual freedom; and with the entire planet bottom-heavy with people under twenty-five—there could be no doubt that the size and drama of this worldwide urban sexual energy was unparalleled.[10]

As Garrett indicates, many of the safeguards instituted over the centuries by society to control or channel biological sexual urges through family, religious, and community norms and values were weakened in the late-twentieth century. The pill opened the door of the sexual revolution that made intercourse outside of marriage acceptable to many people since the possibility of becoming pregnant was now greatly reduced. Condoms were available to prevent both pregnancy and disease. Delaying marriage to older ages as more women entered the labor force and increasing emphasis on individual self-fulfillment were contributing factors as well. All these factors combined to promote sexual activity by both sexes.[11]

Sex is a fundamental biological drive and a highly pleasurable physical and mental experience for many—probably most people. In this context, J. Richard Udry asks whether the basic sociological question should be "Why don't they do it?" rather than, "Why do they do it?"[12] Seen from this perspective, sexual abstinence would be unusual because most people would be expected to want sex. However, some people have a stronger sex drive than do others and some also control this drive better. If some people lack sexual motivation or drive, they do not need social controls to inhibit them. One way or another, Udry explains, they will be abstinent. In addition, if they control their sex drive, they are likely to avoid the problems associated with having sex wherever one finds the opportunity. Passion, alcohol, drugs, and peer pressure, however, can weaken controls.

Udry also notes that sexual behavior is an age-specific behavior that is socially prohibited in childhood and early adolescence but permissible at older ages. Social pressures to engage in it increase significantly in adolescence. Sexual behavior therefore differs from criminal practices and insanity: these are always threatening to social order, while sexual activity is not. With the right person and in the right circumstances, sex can be a positive experience for willing partners and socially approved if these partners are married. Furthermore, if the parties willingly consent, are of lawful age, no danger exists of a sexually-transmitted disease, pregnancy is not an issue, and the sex act is not illegal (e.g., prostitution), there is usually no victim.[13]

In situations where one party is underage or unwilling and force and coercion are used, sex can result in serious emotional problems for the person who is sexually abused or taken advantage of, especially in cases of rape or incest. While illegal sexual activities can and do spread sexual diseases, they are not the major cause of the massive explosion in sexually-transmitted diseases in the late-twentieth century. The causes are, as Garrett indicated, the widespread availability of the birth control pill for women, a greater social atmosphere of permissiveness, geographical separation of husbands and wives in developing countries, and especially the availability of multiple-sex partners. In their major nationwide study of sexuality in the United States, Edward Laumann and his colleagues conclude: "The number of sex partners is the most succinct measure of the extent of exposure to infection."[14] Garrett arrives at a similar conclusion for the world in general:

> At the top of the list [of the causes of infectious diseases] in the 1990s has to
> be sex: specifically, multiple-partner sex. The terrifying pace of the emer-
> gences and reemergences of sexually-transmitted diseases all over the world
> since World War II is testimony to the role that highly sexually active indi-
> viduals, or places of sexual activity, play in amplifying microbial emergences
> such as HIV-1, HIV-2, and penicillin-resistant gonorrhea.[15]

Currently, the ten most frequently reported infectious diseases in the
United States are, in order, chlamydia, gonorrhea, acquired immunodeficiency syndrome (AIDS), salmonellosis, hepatitis A, shigellosis, tuberculo-
sis, syphilis, Lyme disease, and hepatitis B. The five STDS—chlamydia, gonorrhea, AIDS, syphilis, and hepatitis B—account for nearly 90 percent of
all cases reported for these ten diseases. More than 12 million cases of these
diseases are reported in the United States every year, making STDS the
greatest infectious disease problem in the nation. However, as discussed
in the first chapter, risk taking is not always a matter of individual choice
(agency); social structural influences also play a role. This is true for STDS
and AIDS, as seen in the influence of race and social class on patterns of
infection.

Patterns of STDS and AIDS:
Race and Class

Although STDS are found among people in all socioeconomic and racial
groups in the United States, it is undeniable that these diseases are concentrated among the poor and racial minorities. African Americans, who
are overrepresented among low-income groups, have by far the highest
rates of STDS.[16] An analysis of national trends in STDS other than AIDS,
for example, shows that blacks have rates of syphilis more than 60 times
greater than non-Hispanic whites and 10 times greater than Hispanics; for
gonorrhea, rates for blacks are 40 times higher than for non-Hispanic
whites and 15 times higher than for Hispanics.[17]

There are no known biological reasons why race should enhance the
risk of STDS or why African Americans would be more at risk. Family instability, poor school performance, and poverty increase the likelihood of
early sexual initiation and are more common among blacks than whites.[18]
But simply being poor and living in socially and economically disadvantaged neighborhoods do not seem to entirely explain things: the same
number of Hispanics are also poor but have less family instability and

lower STD rates than African Americans. While poverty, broken families, joblessness, minimal access to health care, and a reluctance to seek treatment for STDS because of stigma are key factors in the spread of STDs among African Americans, racial segregation appears to be especially significant. Edward Laumann and Yoosik Youm believe that blacks have the highest rates of STDS because of the "intra-racial network effect."[19] They argue that blacks are more segregated than other racial/ethnic groups in American society and that race tends to structure sexual partnerships. If blacks usually choose other blacks as partners, STDS introduced within this smaller racial group—whose most disadvantaged members are concentrated in socially isolated, low-income, inner-city neighborhoods and rural counties—spread more rapidly than similar infections in the white population. Consequently, the high number of sexual contacts between an infected black core and its periphery of as yet uninfected black sexual partners promotes infection within the black population. Laumann and Youm determined that even though a peripheral (uninfected) African American has only one sex partner, the possibility of that partner being from a core (infected) group is five times higher than it is for peripheral whites and four times higher than for peripheral Hispanics.

An example of the intra-racial HIV network among African Americans is described in Greenwood, Mississippi, by Sack:

> In the first half of 1999, for instance, health officials untangled a trail left by two H.I.V.-positive men in Greenwood who had sex with 18 women over a three-year period. Two of the women had had sex with both men. Five were themselves infected with the virus, and they in turn had had sex with 24 other men.[20]

The racial pattern for HIV/AIDS is similar to that of STDS. For males, Centers for Disease Control and Prevention (CDC) data for 2000–01 show that non-Hispanic blacks have the highest rates of AIDS infection, 106.7 cases per 100,000 population, followed by Hispanics with 42.8, Native Americans/Alaska Natives 18.3, non-Hispanic whites 13.5, and Asian/Pacific Islanders 7.4. For females, non-Hispanic blacks also have the highest rates at 46.1 cases per 100,000 population in 2000-01; Hispanics are next at 11.2, followed by Native Americans/Alaskan Natives (6.1), non-Hispanic whites (2.2), and Asian/Pacific Islanders (1.5). Most women become infected by the AIDS virus (HIV) from either IV drug use or sexual relations with men who are either bisexual, IV drug users, or both. At the beginning of the AIDS epidemic, in the mid-1980s, those infected in the United States were principally non-Hispanic white homosexual males. This pattern, however, altered significantly and the magnitude of the epidemic shifted to African Americans and to a lesser degree Hispanics.

Table 2-1

Mortality Rates for Human Immunodeficiency Virus (HIV) Disease, United States, 1987, 1995, 2000

	(DEATHS PER 100,000 POPULATION)		
	1987	1995	2000
Males			
Non-Hispanic White	10.7	18.0	3.8
Black	26.2	90.4	35.1
American Indian/Native Alaskan	*	11.6	3.5
Asian/Pacific Islander	2.5	6.3	1.2
Hispanic	18.8	42.0	10.6
Females			
Non-Hispanic White	0.5	1.8	0.7
Black	4.6	24.7	13.2
American Indian/Native Alaskan	*	*	1.0
Asian/Pacific Islander	*	0.7	0.2
Hispanic	2.1	9.0	2.9

Source: *Health, United States, 2003* (Washington, DC: U.S. Government Printing Office, 2003).

Table 2-1 shows the mortality rates for HIV for three selected years: 1987, 1995, and 2001. Table 2-1 depicts mortality rates for HIV for non-Hispanic white males rising from 10.7 deaths per 100,000 in the general population in 1987 to 4 per 100,000 in 2001. Black males have the highest death rates, with a rate of 89.0 in 1995, followed by a steep decline to 33.8 in 2001. While these figures represent an obvious improvement, black male mortality from HIV remains the highest of any gender and racial group. Hispanic males had a mortality rate of 40.8 in 1995, but 2001 figures show a decline to 9.7 per 100,000. Native Americans/Alaskan Natives had mortality rates of 4.2 per 100,000 in 2001, while the lowest rates are those of Asians/Pacific Islanders at 1.2.

For females, Table 2-1 shows that black females have far higher mortality rates from HIV than all other groups, even though deaths for this population declined from 24.4 deaths per 100,000 in 1995 to 13.4 in 2001. During the same period, HIV mortality rates for Hispanic females declined from 8.8 in 1995 to 2.7 in 2001. Meanwhile, female HIV mortality has been negligible among non-Hispanic whites, Native Americans/Alaskan Natives, and Asians/Pacific Islanders. While the number of AIDS cases and mortality rates in the United States started to decline in the mid-1990s, the reversal came later and has been much slower for black women, especially for those in the South. In states like Mississippi and North Carolina, more black women than white men have contracted HIV. Initially, the epidemic centered among women in the urban Northeast, drug users who were infected through using contaminated needles, but it is now most frequently seen in heterosexual black women in the South who are infected through sexual intercourse.

However, as previously noted, race per se is not the reason why men and women risk acquiring sexually-transmitted diseases. The link between race and disease is socioeconomic status in that many racial minority persons are also poor and therefore their exposure is greater. Being poor means having less of the good things in life and more of the bad ones, including more health problems like STDS. Affluent African Americans are not similarly burdened with sexual diseases. It is the overrepresentation of particular minorities at the bottom of society that makes race important in the transmission of STDS and AIDS.

Regarding class-based patterns of sexual behavior, abundant research literature shows lower- and working-class people having their first sexual experience at earlier ages and sex with more partners than people in the classes above them.[21] Not surprisingly, there are higher rates of sexual diseases in these lower classes. Yet it is also clear that the sexual behavior of middle- and upper-class individuals is changing as greater sexual permissiveness has spread throughout society.

But the capability to avoid pregnancy and combat sexual disease is also greater at the upper end of the social scale, and members of higher-social strata are not as likely to be in social settings where the probabilities of infection are high. People, of course, do not become infected with STDS and AIDS just because they are poor, but being poor places people in a social environment where they are significantly more likely to be exposed to sexual diseases. Consider, for example, the following description of a scene in a bar in Haiti where low-paid male sugar cane workers go to socialize with prostitutes:

> A syncopated twang blasts through the open-air bar of Jhonnys Patio, as couples embrace and twirl under a flashing rainbow of lights. There is a forced festiveness to the scene, a payday party where men—single and married alike—dance and drink with prostitutes surrounded by murals of nudes.

According to government estimates, as many as 80,000 people earn a living as sex workers in Haiti, and 4.5 to 13 percent of them may be infected [with AIDS]. In Puerto Plata, a resort town on the northern coast, sex is for sale at places ranging from upscale clubs to car washes.[22]

The best odds for avoiding exposure to AIDS during unprotected sex with these prostitutes are one in twenty while the worst odds are about one in ten. This is like playing Russian roulette in that it is just a matter of time until one is hit by the bullet. The question that begs an answer is "Why would someone knowingly risk infection considering these odds or any odds for that matter?" This question will be examined in the next section.

Risking STDS and AIDS

Thus far, this chapter has identified several risk factors in the spread of STDS and AIDS: racial minority status, lower-socioeconomic status, a social climate of permissiveness, reduced fears of pregnancy, geographical separation of spouses in developing countries, and multiple-sex partners. We also know that sexual activity has increased among American adolescents in recent years and that this group is particularly at risk for unsafe sex practices.[23] These practices include multiple partners and irregular birth control/condom use. Poor school performance, alcohol use, and low monitoring by parents are also relevant predictors of adolescent sexual risk taking. Lack of knowledge about the consequences of unsafe sex is a major risk factor for both adolescents and adults that has not yet been mentioned. Persons at the bottom of the social ladder, especially those with little education, are less likely to know about the risk of STDS. David Gonzalez reports from Haiti that the AIDS epidemic there "is terrible not merely in its presence, but also in the ignorance that surrounds it."[24] The brother of one AIDS patient, for example, told Gonzalez that he had died from a spell cast by a creditor. Some people said they did not believe AIDS exists, while volunteer health workers in a small community insisted that no one in their town was infected with the disease, something that was highly unlikely—given the large number of cases in the area. As these examples indicate, lack of knowledge and tendencies toward denial clearly promote the potential for infection.

Knowledge About the Risk of Unsafe Sex

In the United States, where knowledge about the risk of STDS and AIDS should be widespread, a study of nearly 6,000 young homosexual and bisexual men found that 573 were HIV-positive and 77 percent of those infected were unaware of it.[25] These individuals believed they were at low risk of contracting HIV, despite the fact they engaged frequently in the high-risk sexual practice of unprotected anal intercourse. Other studies show the same results.[26] People have unsafe sex that puts them at risk even though they know about safe sex. According to Robert Klitzman, knowledge about the risks has never been shown to be enough to deter a person from unsafe sex.[27] When it comes to sex, Klitzman observes, people do dumb things and this is especially true when alcohol and drugs are part of the experience. Judgment can be seriously impaired under such circumstances.

Tim Rhodes and Linda Cusick, for example, interviewed several people in Great Britain who were HIV-positive and found that many of them tried to abdicate responsibility for placing someone else at risk of HIV transmission by blaming the circumstances they were in—namely, drunkenness or being high on drugs.[28] As one HIV-positive homosexual male in this study reported: "I've done things when I've been drunk or mainly on drugs that I wouldn't have done if I hadn't been on them. It does impair my better judgement."[29] Another told the researchers:

If you use drugs or any sort of drug then actually your standards are lower and you start going to bed with like the ugliest of people because you think they're absolutely gorgeous looking, and you can't actually put any real depth onto the fact that you definitely had safer sex didn't you, because you can't remember, or you can't seem to remember.[30]

But these "self-reports" do not fully explain why people would put themselves in such a risky situation in the first place. Some may take such a risk only once or they may take it several times. Such individuals do this not only because they are high on drugs or alcohol, but also because they are in love, the circumstances seem safe, they trust their partner, or simply because they feel like abandoning caution in the euphoria of the moment. An example of the latter situation is reported by Rhodes who records the following account by a male drug user of sex with his HIV-positive female partner.[31]

Sometimes we decided to spoil ourselves and have real [unprotected] sex. . . . We both decided to throw caution to the wind and have real sex for once, and we enjoyed it all the more although we both knew we were putting me at risk.[32]

Rhodes explains that in this case the risk or costs of unprotected sex did not outweigh the perceived benefits of enhanced sexual pleasure and displays of love, trust, commitment, or permanency in the relationship. Rather, both partners viewed their behavior as normal within a serious relationship. Unprotected sex thus had a symbolic value in communicating commitment and was a rational decision by the two parties, although it could be successfully argued that it was a stupid thing for the uninfected partner to do. Of course, it should be noted that the male drug user injected heroin regularly and so to him the more immediate risk was death due to an overdose, not AIDS. In this situation, the risk of AIDS was secondary to that of dying from a heroin overdose that could happen at any time. It would take months or years, in contrast, to die from AIDS. One heroin user indicated he would never think of using someone else's syringes, but could easily go along without using a condom if the woman he was having sex with agreed.

Rhodes makes the important observation that taking risks is not simply a matter of individual choice: it is often negotiated and options are socially organized around the circumstances people are in. This is especially so for sexual intercourse since it requires another person whose cooperation (or forced coercion) is necessary for the act to go forward. Relying on the partner to make the choice was typical for those people who were passive or powerless in managing the risk. One homosexual male, who, not surprisingly became HIV-positive, described his submissive approach to risk management:

> From day to day I would intend to be safe. And then next encounter I would try and be assertive or do whatever you're supposed to do, but when it came to it, it was basically down to the other person. So I would be safe if they wanted to be safe, and if it didn't come up, it didn't come up. . . . I was just unable to do anything, and even at the time, I wouldn't actually be thinking "Shall I say something or not say," I would just go along with it.[33]

Sometimes a partner in the sex act can be carried away by the passion of the moment and find it difficult or impossible to do anything but comply with the demands of the other partner. According to one HIV-positive heterosexual woman:

> I know and he [her boy friend] knows that we're going to get more passionate, and I start saying to him "Get condoms, get condoms," . . . and he goes "Yes, yes, yes," and before I know it, he is inside and we are shagging, you know, and that's the end of it.[34]

Refusal can be made even more difficult when unprotected sex is presented by one partner as the norm and condom use as deviation from the norm. Thus, it is protected sex that is depicted as unnatural. Rhodes and Cusick describe this situation as an example of risk rationality in reverse, in which protected sex is presented as the more irrational or illogical of sexual behaviors and dangerous unprotected sex is portrayed as the natural norm. In Mississippi, Sack found that the HIV-positive black female patients he interviewed had told their doctor that they understood before they were infected that HIV could be transmitted heterosexually and that it was not only gay white men who became infected. One woman even had annual checkups for HIV, but was infected anyway. The women knowingly placed themselves at risk. Sack writes:

> The women often struggle to explain their recklessness. They look down at the floor when asked to discuss their sexual behavior. Even those who had many sexual partners will say that they were choosy, that they had known their partner for years, sometimes for a lifetime, and that they trusted them. Over and over, they say, they just didn't think it could happen to them.
>
> "I just wasn't thinking about no H.I.V., and I wasn't thinking about no AIDS and I wasn't thinking about no pregnancy," [one woman] said. "I was just being hardheaded. I don't know any other way to break it down."
>
> [A woman] with AIDS . . . said she fell into a fast lifestyle after getting divorced in 1987. She said she might have had 30 to 35 partners over the last ten years, and that they only occasionally used condoms. "I guess I just blocked it out of my mind," she said. "I thought I had a good heart so it wouldn't happen to me. I knew it could happen, I guess, but I was just being stupid."[35]

The African-American women in Sack's report do not appear as people seeking thrills by risking sexual diseases. True, there was little to break the tedium and routine of small-town or rural Mississippi life, and little to provide pleasure other than sex. But Sack cites various health-care workers and researchers who believe that the high-stakes risk taking of these women does not make sense until it is viewed within the context of their lives, which were framed by fatalism, faith, and powerlessness. *Fatalism* is a term used to describe the belief that outcomes of situations are determined by external forces in a person's life like fate, luck, chance, or other more powerful people. Several studies show that people in the lower-social classes are more fatalistic than those in the classes above them.[36] This research indicates that many of these people learn through recurrent experiences that they have limited opportunities, that no matter how hard they try they cannot get ahead, and that more powerful people and unpredictable forces control their lives. These beliefs can be realistic perceptions of their position and are most likely reinforced in daily living. This situation is not simply demoralizing; it can also degrade the will and ability to cope with life's problems.

The black women interviewed by Sack had begun sexual activity at an early age, usually with older men, and discovered they had little ability to persuade their partners to use condoms. The women said that the men would "sweet talk" them into not using one, or promise they would use it the "next time." "I just went along with it," one woman reported. When they were teenagers, these women had felt older men knew what they were doing and would take care of them, while in reality the men had had more sex partners and were more likely to have STDS. Many of the women were desperate for money, and although they were not prostitutes, they expected the men they had sex with to contribute something toward paying their rent or buying groceries. To a large degree, these women were dependent on their boyfriends for support and were told by them: "No honey, no money."[37]

Besides being fatalistic about their lack of control over what happened to them, these women had faith (actually a state of denial) that they would not get a sexually-transmitted disease. It might happen to other people, but not to them. But, in fact, they were powerless to change their economic situation and, as noted, dependent on men for what they could provide (i.e., money, affection, companionship). If the men did not want to use condoms, there was nothing these women felt they could do.

Low Self-Control

While a state of dependency is a major factor in the transmission of HIV/AIDS to these women, low self-control is also a factor, as manifested by a reluctance or capacity to either say no or to insist on their sex partner using condoms. But low self-control does not only apply to those who are infected by others, it also describes persons transmitting the infection.

Michael Gottfredson and Travis Hirschi characterize people engaging in consistent wrongful behavior as impulsive, insensitive, and short sighted, self-centered, indifferent, and insensitive to the suffering and needs of others.[38] Such people typically "live in the moment" and disregard the long-term implications of short-term sensation seeking. They often smoke, drink to excess, have indiscriminate sex, and tend to make poor spouses, friends, and employees. Gottfredson and Hirschi identify low self-control as the key variable associated with wrongful behavior—regardless of the type of behavior or culture in which it is committed. People with high self-control are less likely under all circumstances to commit an illegal or harmful act, unlike people with low self-control, especially those who seek immediate gratification from the act. Gottfredson and Hirschi's research therefore suggests that the key difference in people who knowingly spread sexual diseases is the short-sighted pursuit of self-interest coupled with an absence of self-control that causes them to feel little or no concern about the consequences of their acts. Of course, not everyone with low self-control commits crimes, spreads STDS, and causes problems for society. Some are victims, like the women in Sack's report.

Therefore, as illustrated by Figure 1-1 and previously discussed in Chapter 1, risk responses operate on a continuum of control. Risk responses are (1) passive denial, (2) passive acceptance, (3) active acceptance, and (4) active seeking—each determined by the degree of control from low to high that the individual has over the risk situation. Overall, the risk of a sexual disease is greater for those with low control engaging in either passive denial or passive acceptance. The Mississippi women in Sack's report are examples of passive denial, and their capacity to protect themselves from sexual diseases is negligible. As health psychologist Albert Bandura argues: "Translating health knowledge into effective self-protection action against AIDS infection requires social skills and a sense of personal power to exercise control over sexual situations."[39]

Sex Workers: Dealing with Risks

Commercial sex workers in India, other parts of Asia, and some African countries likely engage in passive acceptance of the risk of sexually-transmitted diseases because they may have little control at best over their sexual transactions. Sex workers elsewhere are more likely to engage in active acceptance since their work exposes them to STDS and HIV/AIDS, but they have some control over their services. A recent study of female sex workers in Tijuana, Mexico, showed that a majority refused requests for oral and anal sex and usually did not negotiate condom use.[40] If the client refused to use a condom, he was refused service. But many of these women also did not like condoms, with some engaging in unprotected sex on occasion in return for a higher fee. These sex workers had been attracted to the commercial sex business because of financial need and were able to earn enough money to take care of themselves and their families if they had one. While few had husbands, some had children who required financial support. The best part of their work was the money the women earned. The worst aspects of their jobs were the risks associated with working in the sex industry—the potential of sexual disease, social stigma, and the possibility of harm from an aggressive or drunk client.

Teela Sanders studied the female indoor sex market in a large British city.[41] These women worked in licensed saunas, brothels, or for escort services in contrast to the women in the Tijuana study who were streetwalkers. Both groups of sex workers, however, confronted the same risks of sexually-transmitted diseases, violence, and social stigma. Sanders found that the British women prioritized their risks along a continuum, somewhat similar to that shown in Figure 1-1. Their risk-continuum from low to high was based on the perceived consequences of the risk and the degree of control they had over minimizing the likelihood of the risk occurring. Health-related matters were a major concern to many, especially the risk of STDS and HIV/AIDS. But these risks were given a low priority compared with other risks because all the women used condoms with clients for all sexual acts and regularly visited health-care specialists to make sure they were not infected. Sanders found that women in the indoor sex markets vehemently insisted on safe sex with their customers. Health risks were therefore considered one of the more straightforward and manageable risks they faced. Sanders states:

> . . . health risks were not considered the most destructive type of occupational hazard for the following reasons. First, most women believed and said it was their experience, that clients who purchase commercial sex from indoor markets were usually compliant with the discourses of safe sex and were willing to accept the "house rules" of the establishment and the personal rules of the workers. Second, and related to the first rationalisation, sex workers maintained that men who wanted unprotected sex would go to the street market where they were more likely to find women willing to barter for high prices in exchange for non-condom use.[42]

In contrast to health risks, physical violence by dangerous clients was ranked next highest as an occupational hazard. Many, but not a majority, of the women had experienced dangerous encounters with customers—yet all were concerned about potential violence. The women would assess potential danger in face-to-face meetings with clients or over the telephone, and they might have someone nearby during the sexual encounter who would come to their aid if necessary. Some had disabling chemical sprays or weapons like knives on hand. Others told the client they had a boyfriend nearby, even if it were not true, and usually this strategy worked. Women employed by escort services would have a driver accompany them to a meeting with the client in case there might be trouble.

All the women had learned what type of client would likely not honor the "contract" between them, and these men were avoided. Using their experience, the women applied their own rules to reject men on the basis of age, ethnicity, dress, accent, appearance, and perhaps the type of car they drove, or if they had bad experiences with such men in the past. Robbery was another potential risk and was usually handled by taking the client's money, leaving the room, and placing it in a safe place before returning to have sex. In the words of one sex worker:

> I let them in, take the money off them, tell them to get undressed. I go out of the room, get my condom and put my money away and come back in the room and do 'em.[43]

The greatest risk and the one that demanded the most strategic thinking and planning was the emotional consequences of selling sex. According to Sanders, there were three potentially powerful emotional risks associated with commercial sex: (1) the emotional implications of managing sex as work and sex as pleasure, (2) the threat of being discovered working as a prostitute by family and friends, and (3) the potential failure of emotional management strategies. After using their body as a commodity, to be purchased for use by a client who was often a stranger, the women had difficulty maintaining private sexual relationships with boyfriends or husbands. Sanders found that one way these women resisted threats to personal relationships was by creating separate meanings for sex at work and sex at home. One woman explained:

> When you are working you are having sex, you are not making love you are having sex . . . so when you go back in your personal relationship you are doing the same but putting feelings to it, so it is not the same.[44]

Other strategies were not allowing clients to kiss them on the mouth or limiting access to parts of their bodies, such as their backside.

Many female sex workers found it impossible to have private sexual relationships. They did not want to engage in sex at work and come home and do it again. One woman who was part of a study of sex workers in Australia stated:

> Well, I'm not going to see eight clients for the night and have to go home and bonk. I need my rest. I like my own bed. Yeah, I don't need the pressure of having to perform in my own bed.[45]

Often private relationships would be terminated by the male partner who could not separate sexual activity at home from what the woman did at work. The demands of sex work were increasingly at odds with both partners' expectations of intimate relationships. One woman in the Australian study reported that her male lover became increasingly cold toward her and eventually admitted he could not handle what she did at work. He said it was hard. Another woman said:

> If you are not in the mood for sex that night [he'll say] "Oh, did you get enough at work?" [or] "Did you have a good run at work?" "I've been woken up in the middle of the night [by my man wanting sex] and you just feel like "Please, just give me a break!"[46]

Most of the sex workers in the British study kept their job hidden from their family, even if they were married. This was very difficult because they could not discuss what happened with their clients and had to constantly worry whether anyone suspected or whether they would meet someone they knew at work in their private life. They had to hide everything connected with work, like money, condoms, lingerie and other clothing, their daily routine, or friendships they had there. The risk of discovery was a continuing anxiety and a 24-hour preoccupation. Whether they were found out was often out of their control, although the women tried to minimize this outcome by working in indoor sex markets or parts of town where family members were not likely to go. The consequences of being discovered were severe, since it could seriously, perhaps permanently, damage the relationships the women wanted to protect. As one woman confided:

> I have to hide it [sex work] all the time: my clothes, where I am going, my health, the way I look after my body. If he [husband] knew, then he would suspect and that would be it, marriage finished.[47]

At times, emotional defenses would fail for some women as the risks associated with commercial sex work overcame their ability to cope with their circumstances. Sanders found that not all women were proficient in avoiding psychological damage. Some developed serious emotional problems. Those with the strongest negative emotions about their work often reacted with low self-esteem and high use of drugs and alcohol. The women hooked on drugs were in an especially bad situation because they sold sex to buy drugs and then depended on these drugs to get them through the experience of having sex with strangers. From his data, Sanders concludes that risk behavior "in prostitution cannot only be understood from a medical or epidemiological viewpoint as the wider social and cultural circumstances of sex workers' lives are as important to their well-being in their understanding of what is a risky outcome."[48] Problems with secrecy, privacy, personal intimate relationships, self-esteem, and a positive social identity are all part of the consequences of being a sex worker.

College Students: Dealing with Risks

While it is doubtful that people with high-control actively seek the risk of STDS or HIV/AIDS, people other than sex workers engage in active acceptance of sexual risks if they routinely choose to pursue an unprotected promiscuous lifestyle. This mode of risk taking is seen in recent research on the sexual behavior of students at a Canadian university. According to Nancy Netting and Matthew Burnett, about 10 percent of these students belonged to a free experimentation subculture that faced the highest risk of HIV/AIDS on campus.[49] People in this group did not use condoms all the time, but their sexual lifestyle involved multiple partners, risky sexual acts, and frequent drug and alcohol use. About 30 percent of the students belonged to a celibacy subculture that was most fearful of the danger of infection. Some males in this group said they lacked the opportunity to engage in sexual intercourse, while others indicated they were not looking for a partner or were waiting to meet the right person. The females were either waiting for love and/or marriage or were fearful of the consequences (e.g., HIV/AIDS, STDS, pregnancy) of sexual intercourse. Some 60 percent had monogamous sexual relationships that relied on love and fidelity—more than condoms—to protect them. Netting and Burnett commented on this group:

> Since most college students are well-informed about the causes and effects of AIDS, the problem is not a lack of knowledge. Rather, it appears that couples stop using condoms when partners know each other well, share strong loving feelings, and/or commit themselves to monogamy. Unfortunately, they rarely have objective knowledge of each other's HIV status, or even their own, and thus are not as safe as they think.[50]

The "free experimenters" had sex less frequently than couples in a monogamist relationship, but they were, as noted, at greatest risk. This was because they had highest number of sexual partners and they used condoms inconsistently. Additionally, they asked the fewest questions about a partner's sexual history. Netting and Burnett state:

> . . . the free experimenters were incautious. Members of this subculture rarely inquired about a potential partner's sexual history, seldom changed their mind about engaging in sex (on those rare occasions when sexual history was discussed), and spent the shortest amount of time getting to know someone before beginning sexual relations.[51]

Celibates, conversely, spent the greatest amount of time getting to know the other person, insisted on knowing about the person's past sexual activities, and most frequently changed their minds about engaging in sex based on the information acquired. Monogamists were cautious also, but not as thorough as the celibates in investigating a potential partner's sexual history. The meaning of sexuality for each group was as follows:

> Celibates appeared to believe that sex was an expression of love and permanent commitment. Monogamists shared this view, but also acknowledged that sex between committed partners could be recreational and serve as a means of physical gratification. In contrast, free experimenters placed almost no emphasis on intimacy, viewing sex primarily as a means of physical gratification. For them, love and sex seemed almost entirely independent.[52]

Conclusion

The sex act is generally a repetitive and potentially joyful occasion over much of the life course. The manner, frequency, and style of participation become part of a person's sexual lifestyle. The decision to risk or not risk sexually-transmitted diseases is an aspect of that lifestyle as well. The evidence suggests that a lifestyle susceptible to risky sex consists of one or more of the following practices: (1) multiple sex partners, (2) non or infrequent use of condoms with these partners, or (3) problem drinking and/or drug use that adversely affects judgment. As Laumann and his colleagues point out: it is risky partners and risky practices that increase the rates of infectivity for sexual diseases.[53] The people most likely to incorporate risky sexual practices into their lifestyle pattern can be from any social class or race, but are most typically adolescents and young adults with low levels of education and income living in poor and racially segregated inner-city or rural areas. These conditions are not at all limited to African Americans, but at this point in time this population group has greater exposure to these circumstances.

Especially critical is a personality tendency toward immediate self-gratification and a disregard of future consequences. The desire for immediate sexual gratification driven by physical arousal and perhaps stimulated by opportunity, the process of seduction, alcohol, drugs, or some other influence, serves to induce the individual in a permissive environment to take the risk. The strength of the person's sex drive in this situation and his or her ability to control that drive and reject the opportunity for sex are significant intervening variables. Conversely, a false trust in the partner or dependent status can undermine objections to sexual risk taking. Ultimately, the outcome of the risk situation is determined by the perceived physical necessity of having sex at that moment, the incentive provided by the partner, the judgment exercised by both parties, and their relationship. As noted, STDS and HIV/AIDS is a disease of society in its most profound and aberrant sense. Risking exposure is a social act influenced by social situations and conditions. Those persons with the lowest degree of control over their sexual encounters are usually at greatest risk, as well as those who seek out risky situations and impose their desires on others indiscriminately.

Notes

1. Allan M. Brandt. 1985. *No Magic Bullet*. New York: Oxford University Press.
2. Goffman, Erving. 1963. *Stigma: Notes on the Management of a Spoiled Identity*. Englewood Cliffs, NJ: Prentice-Hall.

3. Kevin Sack. 2001. "Epidemic Takes Toll on Black Women." *New York Times*, July 3, p. A1, A12.

4. Ibid., p. A12.

5. Betsy L. Fife and Eric R. Wright. 2000. "The Dimensionality of Stigma: A Comparison of Its Impact on the Self of Persons with HIV/AIDS and Cancer." *Journal of Health and Social Behavior*, 41: 50–67.

6. Norbert Elias. 1978. *The Civilizing Process*. New York: Urizen.

7. Bryan Turner. 1996. *The Body & Society*, 2nd ed. London: Sage.

8. Thomas McKeown. 1979. *The Role of Medicine*. Oxford, UK: Blackwell.

9. Laurie Garrett. 1994. *The Coming Plague*. New York: Farrar, Straus, and Giroux.

10. Ibid., p. 263.

11. Edward O. Laumann and Robert T. Michael (eds.). 2001. *Sex, Love, and Health in America: Private Choices and Public Policies*. Chicago: University of Chicago Press.

12. J. Richard Udry. 1988. "Biological Predispositions and Social Control in Adolescent Sexual Behavior." *American Sociological Review*, 53: 709–722.

13. Ibid., p. 710.

14. Edward O. Laumann, John H. Gagnon, Robert T. Michael, and Stuart Michaels. 1994. *The Social Organization of Sexuality*. Chicago: University of Chicago Press.

15. Garrett, p. 610.

16. Institute of Medicine. 1997. *The Hidden Epidemic: Confronting Sexually Transmitted Diseases*. Washington, D.C. National Academy Press; Laumann et al., *The Social Organization of Sexuality*; and Laumann and Michaels (eds.), *Sex, Love, and Health in America*.

17. Institute of Medicine.

18. Karin L. Brewster. 1994. "Race Differences in Sexual Activity Among Adolescent Women: The Role of Neighborhood Characteristics." *American Sociological Review*, 59: 408–424.

19. Edward O. Laumann and Yoosik Youm. 2001. "Racial/Ethnic Group Differences in the Prevalence of Sexually Transmitted Diseases in the United States." In Laumann and Michaels (eds.), *Sex, Love, and Health in America*, pp. 327–351.

20. Sack, p. A12.

21. Laumann and Michaels.

22. David Gonzalez. 2003. "As AIDS Ravages Caribbean, Governments Confront Denial." *New York Times*, May 18, p. 10.

23. Kim S. Miller, Rex Forehand, and Beth A. Kotchick. 1999. "Adolescent Sexual Behavior in Two Ethnic Minority Samples: The Role of Family Variables." *Journal of Marriage and Family*, 61: 85–98; Kathleen Boyce

Rodgers. 1999. "Parenting Processes Related to Sexual Risk-Taking Behaviors of Adolescent Males and Females." *Journal of Marriage and Family*, 61: 99–109.

24. Gonzalez, p. 10.

25. D. MacKellar, L. Valleroy, and G. Secura et al. 2002. "Unrecognized HIV Infection, Risk Behavior, and Mis-Perception of Risk Among Young Men Who Have Sex with Men—6 U.S. Cities, 1994–2000." Barcelona, Spain: 14th International AIDS Conference.

26. Robert Klitzman. 1997. *Being Positive: The Lives of Men and Women With HIV*. Chicago: Dee.

27. Ibid.

28. Tim Rhodes and Linda Cusick. 2001. "Accounting for Unprotected Sex: Stories of Agency and Acceptability." *Social Science and Medicine*, 55: 211–226.

29. Ibid., p. 215.

30. Ibid., p. 216.

31. Tim Rhodes. 1997. "Risk Theory in Epidemic Times: Sex, Drugs and the Social Organisation of 'Risk Behaviour.'" *Sociology of Health and Illness*, 19: 208–227.

32. Ibid., p. 215.

33. Rhodes and Cusick, p. 217.

34. Ibid., p. 218.

35. Sack, p. A12.

36. William C. Cockerham. 2003. *Sociology of Mental Disorder*, 6th ed. Upper Saddle River, NJ: Prentice-Hall.

37. Sack, p. A12

38. Michael R. Gottfredson and Travis Hirschi. 1990. *A General Theory of Crime*. Stanford, CA: Stanford University Press.

39. Albert Bandura. 1989. "Perceived Self-Efficacy in the Exercise of Control over AIDS Infection." In V. Mays, G. Albee, and S. Schneider (eds.), *Primary Prevention of AIDS: Psychological Approaches*. Newbury Park, CA: Sage, p. 129.

40. Jesus Bucardo, Shirley J. Semple, Miguel Fraga-Vallejo, Wendy Davila, and Thomas L. Patterson. 2004. "A Qualitative Exploration of Female Sex Work in Tijuana, Mexico." *Archives of Sexual Behavior*, 33: 343–351.

41. Teela Sanders. 2004. "A Continuum of Risk? The Management of Health, Physical and Emotional Risks by Female Sex Workers." *Sociology of Health and Illness*, 26: 557–574.

42. Ibid., p. 562.

43. Ibid., p. 564.

44. Ibid., p. 567.

45. Deborah J. Warr and Priscilla Pyett. 1999. "Difficult Relations: Sex Work, Love and Intimacy." *Sociology of Health and Illness,* 21: 295.
46. Ibid., p. 297.
47. Sanders, p. 568.
48. Ibid., p. 571.
49. Nancy S. Netting and Matthew L. Burnett. 2004. "Twenty Years of Student Sexual Behavior: Subcultural Adaptations to a Changing Health Environment." *Adolescence,* 39: 19–38.
50. Ibid., p. 21.
51. Ibid., P. 32
52. Ibid., p. 34.
53. Laumann et al., p. 391.

Alcohol

The purpose of this chapter is to consider why people risk becoming alcoholics. People drink alcohol for basically these reasons: (1) they like the taste and/or the way it makes them feel, (2) it facilitates social interaction, (3) it makes their feelings of anxiety and stress disappear, or (4) some combination thereof. The problem arises when they allow their behavior and body physiology to become adversely affected by drink. For example, one male alcoholic, a middle-aged printer, describes his drinking situation:

> The boss says Frank you've got to quit. I try, but you know I get those shakes in the morning on the way to work. I stop and get a half-pint of Peppermint Schnapps, so they can't smell it on my breath, and I drink it and then I quiet down, start to smile, and feel good. It starts to wear off about the middle of the morning. That's why I keep the cold beer in the ice chest in the trunk of the car. I go out for a smoke and sneak a beer. That gets me through to noon. Then I take lunch at Buddies and have a couple shots of Schnapps, with the beer that everyone else has. I can make it through the afternoon. Then I stop after work and really hit it. I get so shook up about not being able to stop that I seem to drink more. I keep drinkin till I pass out every night. . . . My body's starting to show the effects now. The Doc says the liver can't take too much more of this. I don't know, when I take that drink these problems all go away. But they're there when the drink wears off.[1]

Some people and organizations, including Alcoholics Anonymous (AA), claim that alcoholism is a disease and that heavy drinkers should be defined as "sick" and in need of treatment. This perspective makes the alcoholic a "victim," rather than a "culprit." The drinking alcoholic is viewed as powerless in the presence of alcohol and unable to refrain from drinking. Others disagree. They believe heavy drinkers are responsible for their drinking behavior because they deliberately choose to drink, instead of engaging in some alternative form of behavior.

The question of whether alcoholism is a disease has not been answered, nor it is likely to be until the precise causes are scientifically verified. Furthermore, while no single definition of alcoholism is universally accepted, one developed several years ago by Mark Keller has gained widespread acceptance. Keller skirts the issue of whether alcoholism is a disease or problem of behavior, saying that it can be either. Because there is support for both perspectives, this compromise helps make his definition acceptable to most experts and allows us to move past such a debate and consider what alcoholic behavior actually is. As Keller defines it:

> Alcoholism is a chronic disease, or a disorder of behavior, characterized by the repeated drinking of alcoholic beverages to an extent that exceeds customary dietary use or ordinary compliance with the social drinking customs of the community, and which interferes with the drinker's health, interpersonal relations, or economic functioning.[2]

Alcohol Use and Misuse: An Overview

Ethyl alcohol is a drug, which in both type and degree of effects is intermediate between habit-forming and addicting drugs. Alcoholic beverages of one type or another have been known and imbibed for centuries, with the first alcoholic drink generally believed to be mead (made from water, honey, malt, and yeast) appearing as early as the Paleolithic Age around 8000 B.C. Today, alcohol is consumed in a variety of liquid forms like beer, wine, and liqueurs, or as distilled spirits such as vodka, scotch, gin, rum, and bourbon. These beverages are products of the fermentation of various fruits, especially grapes, or sugar cane, or the malting or distillation of potatoes or cereal grains like wheat, corn, and barley.

Alcohol: Physiological Effects

Although the effects of alcohol on the body have been well-studied, the exact mechanisms that produce them have not been conclusively identified. The best evidence to date suggests that once alcohol enters the stomach, it requires no digestion, with most of it absorbed unchanged into the small intestine, except for a certain amount that enters the bloodstream where it is carried first to the liver and then to all parts of the body in a diluted state. The principal action of alcohol within the body is to depress the functioning of the brain, reducing the effectiveness and integrated performance of the central nervous system. Alcohol apparently affects the neuronal membrane by inhibiting the ability of a neuron to transmit information. This depressant action affects brain function in much the same way as an anesthetic, such as chloroform or ether.

The degree of the brain's impairment depends on the amount of alcohol present in the bloodstream, as determined by the type of alcoholic drink and the proportion of alcohol it contains, how quickly it is drunk, the amount and type of food in the stomach, and various minor physiological differences among people. The social setting where the alcohol is consumed and the psychology of the drinking situation can also influence the manner in which an intoxicated person overtly expresses his or her behavior and the degree of intoxication.

Although alcohol is often believed to be a stimulant, it is not; it is, as noted, a depressant. The reason that some people regard alcohol as a stimulant is because the behavior of inebriated people appears to be stimulated rather than depressed. But what actually occurs is that the exaggerated behavior that accompanies drinking too much alcohol more resembles releasing a brake than stepping on an accelerator. Some people become hostile, aggressive, amorous, or perhaps passive and withdrawn—depending on their personality, the drinking environment, and their own personal mode of adjusting to alcohol's effect on their nervous system.

Consumed in moderate quantities, alcohol may have little effect on overt behavior and even diminish feelings of tension, anxiety, and fatigue. Moderate amounts consumed regularly, especially red wine, have been shown to reduce the risk of cardiovascular disease.[3] Alcohol can also promote feelings of well-being. Seldon Bacon refers to the relief of anxiety as alcohol's "easing" function because it offers an "easing" of situations in which a person may believe that he or she may be somewhat ineffective or poorly prepared to deal with.[4] Bacon suggests that, provided drinking is not unpleasant, the "easing" function may operate for all drinkers.

Whereas moderate drinking is not generally regarded as harmful, excessive consumption can grossly disturb the cerebral cortex's control over a person's actions to the extent that physical coordination, emotion, and behavior are severely affected. The sensitivity of the brain to cues, its ability to recognize the environment, process information, make decisions, send information to other parts of the body, and the quality of bodily and motor responses are altered. In addition to the problems of adjusting to the immediate effects of alcohol on the brain and coping with drunkenness, the person who has indulged in the continued excessive consumption of alcohol over time has greatly increased the likelihood of physical damage to his or her body. Such damage may be the direct result of alcohol's toxic effects that are associated with gastric ulcers and, in combination with nutritional deficiencies, can cause certain blood disorders and liver damage. Excessive drinking also promotes an early death from cirrhosis of the liver, heart disease, stroke, alcohol poisoning, heart attacks from binge drinking, and diseases like pneumonia and diabetes that are strengthened because of the body's alcohol-weakened defenses.

Additionally, there are substance-related mental disorders caused by alcohol or drug abuse that produce behavior considered maladaptive or undesirable in most cultures, as well as impairment in social or work functioning, an inability to control the use of the substance, and development of severe withdrawal symptoms after cessation of use. Substance-related disorders are divided into substance-use disorders (characterized by dependence and abuse) and substance-induced disorders (characterized by intoxication and withdrawal symptoms). To be diagnosed with a substance-use disorder caused by alcohol, a person must have seriously disturbed relations with other people because of drinking and either a psychological dependence on alcohol or a pathological pattern of use. Pathological patterns of use are characterized by long periods of intoxication, daily or almost daily use, and complications like blackouts and hallucinations as a result of intoxication. Substance-induced disorders stem from the direct effects of the substance on the central nervous system, including symptoms of withdrawal. Diagnoses involving alcohol must show seriously disturbed mental behavior centered on the drinking experience.

The onset of alcoholism tends to occur after 5 to 15 years of heavy drinking. The demarcation line between a "heavy" drinker and an alcoholic is not clear, but the primary factor in being an alcoholic is addiction to/or dependence on alcohol. Most researchers agree that physical withdrawal symptoms (tremors of hands, tongue, and eyelids; nausea; malaise; anxiety; and depressed mood or irritability) are symptoms of such dependence, and alcohol is usually consumed to relieve or avoid them.

Alcohol: Social Problems

Besides the negative physiological effects of excessive alcohol consumption, alcoholism is a serious social problem. Alcohol is the most abused substance in the world. In the United States, over nine million people are estimated to be alcoholics. Some 50 percent of all automobile accidents resulting in a fatality likewise involve drivers who have been drinking, with many having a history of alcohol abuse. The probability of being involved in an accident while under the influence of alcohol is increased the more alcohol that is consumed. As one male alcoholic reported:

> One morning I woke up after a night of drinking, and I thought I had this bad dream about running into the side of a bridge at 55 miles an hour. Then I went outside. Three inches off the side of my car were gone. And I thought, "Man, I've *got* to stop *driving*."[5]

Note the alcoholic did not say he had to stop drinking: he said that he had to stop *driving*. In this instance, no one was injured, but a report of a male driver who was in an accident after consuming too much alcohol shows another outcome:

> . . . [He] had just pulled out to pass a truck when he noticed a car coming toward him. With his reflexes slowed by alcohol, he veered too sharply, got his tires caught in the shoulder of the road, lost control of the car, and crashed head-on into another car. When he regained consciousness several hours later, he learned that one of the two women in the other car had to be rushed to the city for emergency surgery, while the other was in serious condition in the same local hospital he was in with smashed teeth, cracked ribs, a collapsed lung, and a broken leg. A compulsion to make amends overcame him. He dragged his bruised body out of bed and hobbled down the hospital corridor until he found her room. Her husband sat near her bed. He introduced himself to them both, admitting responsibility for the accident, then asked if he could help in any way. They were nice enough, but they did not grant him the absolution he was seeking. As he left the room, he realized he was through drinking.[6]

In addition to the deaths and injuries and health problems caused by excessive alcohol consumption, the economic costs of alcoholism run into billions of dollars because of the lost production of goods and services, worker inefficiency and absenteeism, accidents, cost of health care, and the disability and premature deaths of workers.

Furthermore, the FBI reports that about every third arrest in the United States involves drunkenness and that the majority of all short-term prisoners are in jail for acts committed under the influence of alcohol.[7] Excessive drinking accounts, either directly or indirectly, for about 40 percent of all cases brought before courts with jurisdiction over domestic problems. These cases do not reflect the considerable harm done to individuals and society through the misuse of alcohol resulting in the disturbed children of alcoholic parents, divorce and family disruption, mental anguish, physical pain, personal degradation, loss of friends, alcohol-related suicides, and other negative situations.

Social Patterns of Drinking

Before reviewing the theories and evidence about why people take risks with alcohol, we will examine selected social structural factors that cluster people into particular drinking groups. Religion, for example, plays a significant role in alcohol use in that religious people tend to drink significantly less than those who are not religious. In the United States, religion has a particularly strong influence on promoting abstinence. This influence is especially felt in the South, which historically is the region with the highest proportion of people who abstain from alcohol and the lowest rates of alcoholism in the country.[8] This is not to say that alcohol use is rare in the South because considerable drinking does take place there, just that the proportion of Southerners who drink is smaller than occurs in other regions. Southerners, the majority of whom are conservative Protestants, often hold generally unfavorable attitudes toward alcohol use; even those who drink themselves share the antipathy. The influence of religious beliefs on alcohol consumption is also shown in Utah, which has a large Mormon population and the lowest per capita consumption of alcohol of any state in the United States. Figures for 2002, for example, place Utah last in alcohol consumption, at 1.29 gallons per person.[9] New Hampshire is first, at 4.0 gallons. However, New Hampshire has some of the cheapest prices for alcoholic beverages in New England because of its tax structure, and out-of-state buyers are attracted to the relatively low costs. So it is not clear if all the alcohol purchased there is actually consumed there. A better comparison is Nevada, with its gambling centers that attract large numbers of people, many of them tourists. In Nevada, alcohol is usually consumed locally and, not surprisingly, it has the second highest per capita consumption (3.6 gallons) at the state level. Religion does not appear to be a strong factor in controlling alcohol use in Nevada since people visit the state to enjoy themselves, not practice their religion. In other areas where religiosity is strong, less alcohol is usually consumed.

The largest proportion of drinkers is found among the population in the West, where Nevada, Alaska, Colorado, and Wyoming are among the leading states in alcohol consumption.[10] Nevada, along with the District of Columbia, also reports the most sales of alcohol per capita.[11] Where a person lives can therefore influence drinking habits. Other significant structural variables are age and gender, race, and socioeconomic status, which will be discussed in this section. The point here is that drinking alcohol is not a random event without any connection to the wider society.

Age and Gender

The majority of Americans have their first experience with alcohol during mid-adolescence (15 to 16 years of age), with boys somewhat more likely to try alcohol at an earlier age than girls are. Males consume the greater amount of alcohol, especially in late adolescence and young adulthood. While girls generally drink less than boys, the number of girls who drink increases with age so that by the end of high school most members of both sexes have tried alcohol. Drinking among high school students is so common that those who have not at least tasted it are in a distinct minority.

While most Americans try alcohol during adolescence, the largest proportion of regular drinkers are young adults from 21 to 24 years of age. The largest proportion of abstainers among adults are age 49 and over. For women, the age of heaviest drinking is from 21 to 29 years; for men, the heaviest drinking occurs between ages 18 to 20 and 35 to 39. Men drink in greater numbers and more frequently then women, but since World War II the proportion of both men and women who drink has steadily increased. About 70 percent of all men and half of all women in the United States drink alcohol at least once a month. For both genders, the use of alcohol declines with advancing age, though abuse is not entirely absent among the elderly. Serious drinking problems sometimes persist among some older people as they age and cope with retirement, the deaths of loved ones, loneliness, and other situations they perceive to be negative. But the great majority of elderly are not heavy drinkers.

Race

When racial patterns of alcohol abuse in American society are considered, Native Americans are usually characterized as the ethnic group for whom alcohol has caused the greatest difficulties.[12] Members of this group have high rates of arrests for alcohol-related offenses and high mortality rates for alcohol-specific causes, including accidents like drunk driving. Nationwide surveys show that heavy drinking is more prevalent among Native Americans than any other ethnic group.[13] In many Native-American communities, alcohol is a major contributing factor to a variety of social problems, including poor health, crime, family disorganization, unemployment, and suicide. Nevertheless, the stereotype of the "drunken Indian" is not applicable to all Native Americans and may actually apply only to particular tribes with widespread problem drinking.

There is also extensive drinking among both black and white Americans, but alcohol use may be more prevalent among whites. Research on drinking patterns in the South, for example, shows whites drinking more alcohol than blacks.[14] There are also nationwide studies that report black and white men have similar drinking patterns until age 49, at which time heavy drinking becomes substantially greater among whites.[15] Black women, in contrast, drink less than white women, regardless of age. Black women are also more likely than white women and both black and white men to abstain from drinking altogether. Additionally, blacks appear to be generally more disapproving of drinking and drunkenness than whites.[16] However, the mortality rates for cirrhosis of liver, which is indicative of alcoholism, are slightly higher for blacks than for whites, while rates for Hispanics are even higher and all racial groups trail Native Americans in cirrhosis deaths by a wide margin.

Among whites, Irish Americans are known to have especially high rates of alcohol consumption, a pattern that has continued for generations.[17] In Western Europe, the Irish have the highest overall consumption rates of alcohol. In 2000, for instance, the Irish drank an average of 14.2 liters per capita compared to a European Union average of 9.1 liters. The Irish-American pattern of drinking may therefore be influenced by the broader Irish culture that equates socializing with drink.

As for Hispanic Americans, the degree to which they consume alcohol compared to other ethnic groups has not been fully investigated. Little is known about drinking among female Hispanics. But among Hispanic males, research shows that Puerto Ricans and Mexican Americans have higher rates of drinking than do Cuban Americans.[18] In describing the relationship between race and alcohol, it is clear that drinking by males is widespread across all ethnicities, with the exception of Asian Americans of both genders who often do not drink or drink only in moderation.

Socioeconomic Status

Sociologists have produced substantial evidence that rates of excessive drinking are related to class. One of the earliest studies summarizing community drinking patterns is that by sociologist John Dollard in the 1940s suggesting that members of the upper- and lower-social strata were the most likely to become alcoholics.[19] A fundamental difference between the two social classes, according to Dollard, was that members of the lower class were more likely to engage in uncontrolled heavy drinking and to come to the notice of the police because of it. The upper class, in contrast, gave its members considerable latitude in their drinking behavior, and so they were less likely to get in trouble with law enforcement authorities because their use of alcohol was more private. As one upper-class woman in her mid-30s described her drinking problem:

> I was high-class. I wore the best clothes, went to the best hairdresser, had the best college education, came from high-status parents. My father was the head of a hospital. I had to drink the most expensive scotch in the world. And I did, a fifth a day for 5 years. Then it became a quart, and then I knew something was wrong. Why did it take so much scotch to make me feel good?[20]

This woman blamed the alcohol rather than herself for her increased drinking. But in her upper-class world, contact with the police was unlikely and, in her case, did not occur, since her drinking was private. Dollard found that upper-middle-class persons tended to have relatively neutral attitudes toward drinking; that is, they did not have a strong opinion about it one way or another.[21] They were relatively tolerant of people who imbibed until their behavior became a serious problem for themselves and especially others. Drinking was commonplace among members of this class and a characteristic feature of their social activities. The lower-middle class, in contrast, was strongly opposed to alcohol use; their opposition was part of an overall pattern of respectability. But still many lower-middle-class persons consumed alcohol. Persons in the class below them—the working class—were more likely to drink than those in the lower-middle class, however, and their attitudes toward alcohol use were generally more positive. Male drinking and drunkenness were not unusual in the working class.

Other surveys have continued to find a significant relationship between alcohol consumption and socioeconomic status, but in contrast to Dollard's work, they also find the lower class contains a large number of people who abstain from drinking.[22] Thus, it appears that lower-class drinking patterns are characterized by both the greatest proportion of abstainers and problem drinkers. Problem drinkers are people who cause others difficulties because of their drinking and frequently have encounters with the police because of it. Conversely, the greatest proportion of people who drink is found in the upper-middle and upper classes.

One of the basic indicators of class position is education, and generally it appears that the largest proportion of abstainers in American society exists among persons with an eighth-grade education or less. The proportion of people who drink, however, increases as education rises. Drinking is most common among college graduates, but people with a postgraduate degree tend to drink slightly less than do those with a bachelor's degree.

Heavy Drinking and Alcoholism

Both heavy drinkers and alcoholics drink heavily, but alcoholics are clearly addicted to it. Behavioral and medical scientists generally describe addiction, alcoholic or otherwise, in terms of psychological and physiological dependence, and agree that physical withdrawal symptoms are an integral part of such dependence. Withdrawal symptoms not only result from addiction, but also reinforce it when the alcoholic uses alcohol to alleviate the pain and discomfort of withdrawal. Addiction thus becomes a situation in which a person is emotionally and physiologically dependent on alcohol to a point beyond which he or she can no longer voluntarily control the craving for it.

To summarize the research and various accounts of drinking behavior by alcoholics themselves, the alcoholic is someone who (1) lacks the emotional stamina to refrain from drinking, (2) has a strong mental and physical craving for alcohol, (3) suffers from severe mental and physical withdrawal symptoms when deprived of alcohol, (4) shows signs of physical and emotional deterioration, and (5) can be characterized by his or her relinquishing of all other interests because of the preoccupation with obtaining and consuming alcohol, as shown by the following example:

> Nick's hangovers were spectacular. As he said, the first sensation is blinding pain. It's like what I imagine a brain tumor would feel like. Your head hurts so bad that you cannot even open your eyes. I go to the bathroom and swallow some aspirin but they make me throw up. I go back to bed and wait until I get sick then I rush to the john and have the "dry heaves" for nearly an hour. . . . Then I go back to sleep but I cannot sleep long because I have nightmares, and wake up dying of thirst. A bloody Mary in the morning is the only solution. When I get one I nearly choke on it, but in about five minutes my head comes back to my shoulders and my eyes start to focus again.[23]

Theories of Alcoholism

There are several theories about why people drink to the point where they risk alcoholism and the adversity associated with it. That people would want to risk their health by heavy drinking or alcoholism seems unlikely, yet obviously it happens, since alcohol is the most abused substance in the world. No single theory explains all the varied factors that are symptomatic of the affliction, but current theories nonetheless contribute to our understanding of why some people become alcoholics. The theories discussed here implicate (1) physiological, (2) genetic, (3) psychological and psychiatric, and (4) sociological causes.

Physiological Theories

Several theories about alcoholism can be classified as physiological and reflect the effort by numerous researchers to develop a theory corresponding to a medical model that allows physicians to treat the problem effectively. One of the leading proponents of physiological theories is E. M. Jellinek who argued many years ago that psychological dependence on alcohol was not an addiction.[24] According to this view, addiction can only result from physiological factors. Jellinek identified four stages of drinking behavior. The first stage is the *prealcoholic* stage, in which the drinker moves from social drinking to using alcohol to relieve stress and anxiety. Next is the *prodomal* stage, in which the drinker realizes that alcoholic drinks are not beverages, but drugs; this stage ends with the onset of a loss of control over drinking. Alcohol consumption is heavy during this stage and the drinker, for the first time, experiences "blackouts." The third stage is the *crucial* phase, in which the body's physiological need for alcohol drives the drinker to consume increasingly more alcohol. Finally, there is the *chronic* stage, during which obtaining and consuming alcohol dominates the drinker's daily activities. In this most severe stage, there is also damage to the liver and nervous system accompanied by powerful withdrawal symptoms. Although Jellinek's theory is intriguing, subsequent research has failed to find evidence showing most alcoholics go through the stages he described and found that physiological damage can occur earlier than he claimed.

Another physiological theory states that certain people have a peculiar body chemistry (an allergy) which produces a physiological reaction to alcohol that causes loss of control over drinking. However, there is a lack of supporting evidence for this theory, as well for other theories that attempt to link nutritional deficiencies and drinking. Many alcoholics do suffer from neuroendocrine disorders, but it is not clear whether these are a cause of drinking or an effect. While body physiology is important in understanding alcoholism, other factors should not be sidelined since this approach has yet to provide convincing arguments that physiological defects alone are responsible for alcoholism.

Nevertheless, alcohol does have potent pharmacological effects on body physiology and, as Arnold Ludwig explains, these effects must have a significant role in perpetuating continued drinking. "Almost up to the bitter end," states Ludwig, "even when the euphoric effects of alcohol become more fleeting and short-lived, it can still be relied upon to help the alcoholic feel more 'normal.' "[25] Yet he believes that other factors, beside the addictive aspects of alcohol, need to be taken into account, especially psychological variables that help explain why alcoholics resist warnings and pleas from other people to stop drinking and turn down help when it is offered.

Genetic Theories

Genetic theories of alcoholism hold considerable promise because alcoholism appears to be common in some families and not in others. The children of alcoholic parents, for example, have a much stronger likelihood of becoming alcoholic than do children who have no family history of alcoholism. This does not mean it is a certainty that children of alcoholics will become alcoholics, but they may have a predisposition toward it that needs to be controlled. Thus, there is a strong possibility that some persons may inherit a predisposition toward alcoholism, or, conversely, perhaps immunity to it, but to date research has not conclusively shown this or identified a responsible gene. The situation may change since completion of the Human Genome Project now provides researchers with a map of the human genetic code to further such investigations.

Psychological Theories

Psychological theories of alcoholism and the related field of psychiatry dominate current theorizing about drinking. Research in these areas has firmly established the proposition that many people are motivated to drink to obtain relief from anxiety, worry, fear, frustration, and tension. Efforts have also been made to go beyond the anxiety-relief explanation and seek the causes of heavy drinking in disturbances of the personality or ascertain if drinking is learned behavior. This research has been inconclusive, as have the results of studies looking to identify a particular personality type conducive to alcoholism. Limited evidence suggests that some alcoholics may share a few common personality traits like weak defense mechanisms, low tolerance for tension, and unresolved love-hate conflicts, but it is not clear if these traits predate the onset of alcoholism or are a consequence of excessive drinking. As Ludwig points out, "there is no such thing as a typical alcoholic personality" and "there are also probably as many different innate personality patterns among alcoholics as can be found in the general population."[26]

Learning theory is another approach in psychology to the study of alcoholism. It is based upon the proposition that when a response to a stimulus results in a rewarding situation, the relationship between the stimulus and the response is strengthened. If the response is not rewarded, it will tend to disappear and be replaced by other responses. Learning theory suggests that excessive drinking is a satisfying response to stimuli that produce fear or anxiety. Since alcoholism is known to be unpleasant, the logic of accepting learning theory as a rationale for understanding drinking might seem questionable. But learning theorists explain that alcohol serves the *immediate* purpose of reducing tension and the unpleasant consequences of intoxication appear only later. When alcohol is consumed in association with an emotional state characterized by fear or anxiety, and results in a temporary release from those conditions, learning theorists claim that the emotional state itself can take on the properties of a stimulus, thereby continuing to produce a strong desire to drink. Once the drinking response is established, learning theory holds that its repetition constitutes reinforcement and eventually leads to alcohol addiction.

The merit of using learning theory to understand alcoholism rests on claims that drinking alcohol is a learned behavior. That is, drinking occurs, at least initially in a social context, with other people who condone the consumption of alcohol as a stimulus for increased enjoyment of the interaction taking place or as a way of dealing with one's problems. Drinking thus becomes a socially acceptable response within a particular group, and new group members are socialized accordingly into accepting and participating in the prevailing drinking norms. Often acceptance of drinking as a response to anxiety is perpetuated and reinforced, either directly or indirectly, by a society's culture. For instance, it is not unusual to witness actors (usually male) in films, plays, or on television "have a drink" on being confronted with some particularly threatening situation; this connection of stress to drinking in the media has become so commonplace that its occurrence as an interpretation of reality is seen as ordinary rather than exceptional.

Even with these contributions to the understanding of alcoholism, learning theory is limited in its explanatory power because it is unable to differentiate between learned behavior that results in alcoholism and learned behavior that does not do so. People can learn to drink in specific ways and in particular contexts, but all of them will not become alcoholics. In addition, learning theory fosters an image of human beings in which they have no choice over whether they drink or not; instead, once people find alcohol satisfying, they are presumed to drink in a more or less automatic (or conditioned) fashion when exposed to stimulilike stress. Admittedly, some people may lose control over their drinking to the extent that it may seem to be an automatic response, but for others, the act of drinking may be a much more complex process than simply a conditioned reflex. Some people may just like to drink, but never drink excessive amounts or ever lose control, or ever become alcoholics.

Sociological Theories

Some sociological theories about drinking have made valuable contributions to understanding drinking behavior. Their significance lies in the realization that social relationships and the social context within which alcohol use takes place can determine drinking practices—including the reasons for drinking, the manner in which a person behaves when drinking, and the type, quantity, and frequency of alcohol consumption. An understanding of the social factors involved in drinking can give meaning to the drinking patterns of individuals and groups beyond explanations of physiological and psychological dependence on alcohol.

For example, research in Canada shows that each social setting carries its own rules and norms regarding drinking in terms of appropriateness and choice of beverage, and is as critical as the characteristics of the individual in explaining alcohol intake per occasion. Thus, research on college students showed that they drink more alcohol in group settings, especially parties, while binge drinking occurs mainly on Saturdays with friends when dating partners or spouses are absent.[27] The more students perceive drinking to be the norm in university social activities, the more they drink per occasion, particularly males.

Other research shows wives adjusting their drinking practices to match those of their husbands with respect to frequency of drinking and consumption.[28] Social class, however, makes a major difference in that the higher the social position, the more drinking is integrated into their lifestyle and the more chances the spouses have to drink together and adjust their drinking patterns to each other. Thus, it appears that the people an individual drinks with influence his or her drinking behavior. People tend to drink less in the company of family members, neighbors, and members of their church, but more than usual when with close friends. In addition, a person's drinking companions may influence the type of beverage consumed; for example, hard liquor is consumed more frequently with friends than family. Studies of taverns and bars have been able to identify the social nature of such establishments since they cater to particular clienteles like certain neighborhoods or people of similar ages, class, occupations, race, or sexual orientations. As one woman says:

Well there's Cheers—where everybody knows your name. There's the same crowd in there everyday, so you feel comfortable and you don't have to worry about anything happening.[29]

Another woman explains that different bars have different attributes. Some carry more risk of problems than others, but different bars serve different purposes at different times:

. . . I think certain places have the image of being "meat markets." ["pick-up" bars where you put yourself on display for romance and/or sex] Other places are known . . . if you want to go dancing. . . . Or if you just want to go somewhere to talk, you go somewhere that's not loud. So, I think bars have different characteristics.[30]

The type of drinking experience is thus centered on the type of social interaction peculiar to that setting. There are, of course, several reasons why people go to bars, including companionship, enjoyment, diversion, validation of their self-image as being attractive to others, escape from boredom, and anxiety relief. But whatever the reason for their going, the setting for drinking is a crucial factor in the experience of consuming alcohol. The effects of alcohol are not simply a function of the pharmacological properties of the substance and the individual's level of physical tolerance: they can be fully understood only in the context of the roles, norms, and circumstances of use.[31]

In a major sociological theory of drinking that he proposed during the 1940s, Robert Bales suggested that patterns of alcohol consumption in a society are largely dependent on three major cultural variables.[32] First is the degree to which a culture creates the need to adjust to tension by drinking, since many people drink to relieve anxiety. According to Bales, the less tension generated within a culture, the less alcohol that culture will consume. Second, Bales hypothesized that the attitudes toward drinking produced by a culture are very important, as shown in religious groups espousing abstinence, ceremonial drinking associated with rituals, convivial drinking in which camaraderie is expected, and so on. Such attitudes can set socially-prescribed limits on the amount and type of alcohol consumed, or undo limits if attitudes are permissive. Third, Bales believed that the degree to which a culture provides alternatives to drinking can influence rates of alcoholism. For example, participation in certain religious rituals acts as an alternative to drinking as a means of reducing anxiety. The central relevance of Bales' theory is that cultural differences in drinking are an undoubted social fact. Some groups in society drink more than other groups, while still other groups do not even drink—all depending on their attitudes toward drinking and the culture in which these attitudes develop.

Other sociological explanations of the causes of drinking include Robert Merton's notion of social structure and anomie and Edwin Lemert's concept of primary and secondary deviance. Merton suggests that social structures exert pressure on individuals to engage in nonconforming behavior when there is a rupture between the norms and goals ("the things worth striving for") of a society and the means to reach those goals.[33] This situation produces a state of anomie, or normlessness, because of a mismatch between society's goals and the socially structured means to reach those goals. This situation is most common for members of the lower class who are asked by society to orient their behavior toward the prospect of success but at the same time are denied opportunities to become successful by the social structure because of their class position as seen in their lack of education, money, and job situation. One mode of adaptation, says Merton, is *retreatism*, in which the individual, rejecting both society's goals and means, adapts by turning instead to alcohol. The alcoholic skid-row bum or homeless person is an example of someone who, having retreated from society, becomes an alcoholic in the process.

Lemert's concept of primary and secondary deviance is intended to explain the social consequences of being labeled "an alcoholic."[34] According to Lemert, primary deviance is a situation in which a person acts differently or strangely, but the behavior is rationalized by others as atypical, since it is not perceived as characteristic of the person's true self. Secondary deviance is more serious because it is a situation in which a person is perceived to be deviant because his or her unacceptable behavior is thought to be typical of him or her. Excessive drinking, for example, may be regarded initially as primary deviance since it is not thought to be the frequent behavior of a particular person. But if it then occurs often, that person may be relegated to a position of secondary deviance over time by others who come to define and label him or her as an alcoholic. The person may then find it necessary to locate a group that can accommodate the deviance. Someone labeled by others as an alcoholic, in other words, may be rejected socially by moderate drinkers and abstainers. The person, consequently, may be forced (if he or she desires companionship) to develop associations with other people who drink heavily or who accept alcoholism as normative behavior.

Thus, we have the stereotypical situation of the once socially acceptable person whose heavy drinking eventually leads to a disruption of his or her normal relationships, leading to downward social mobility, as this individual descends into a world of alcoholics and "skid-row" living conditions in which heavy drinking and drunkenness is the norm. Although neither Lemert's nor Merton's concept fully explains alcoholism, they contribute to our understanding of how society causes alcoholics to be viewed as people excluded from normal society.

Finally, there is the research by Norman Denzin on the self-concepts of alcoholics.[35] Denzin found that the alcoholic self is divided against its self. That is, the alcoholic is narcissistic and self-centered, but at the same time engages in self-hatred for being unable to refrain from drinking and having lost control over the craving for alcohol. Because of their being unable to present a true picture of themselves to others and because they view others through an alcoholically-clouded consciousness, alcoholics' emotional, sexual, and social relationships are altered. Alcoholics, says Denzin, live in a distorted world of social relationships characterized by "a maddening inner self-drama that is scripted by resentment and hatred."[36] Self-love and self-hate collide in a way that is self-defeating and damaging to the alcoholic.

Conclusion

Drinking is widespread in American society. Although there are proportionately more drinkers in the upper class, more "problem" drinkers as well as abstainers are found in the lower class. More men drink than women, but the number of women drinkers is increasing. Older teenagers and young adults drink more than other age groups, while drinking significantly decreases in older age groups.

The reasons people give to explain why they take risks with alcohol is that it helps them to relax, relieves tension and anxiety, helps them enjoy themselves, facilitates social interaction, and they like the taste. The anxiety/relief explanation is the reason most often given for drinking in the psychological literature, and ample research supports this finding. As one woman reports:

> My job is stressful. I can see why others in my type of job are alcoholics. Because there are days that the first place I want to head for is a bar. If I don't, I know I am going to kill somebody.[37]

However, the use of alcohol to facilitate social interaction should not be underestimated. Some people drink alcohol even before they go out drinking with other people so they can relax, "loosen up," "be fun to be with," and "get into the mood" from the very beginning of socializing. Alcohol does serve an "easing" function. One of the most perplexing questions about alcohol concerns why certain people are able to stop drinking, while others continue to drink, despite the problems they have with it and the risks to their health. Many people report they want to get a little "tipsy" when drinking but to stay in control. This is how they relax and have fun. But becoming too tipsy and especially drunk is undesirable for many people. They have a particular level of intoxication that they recognize and like to reach, yet tend to slow down, stop drinking altogether, or switch to soft drinks, coffee, or water when they reach this point. Why some people go beyond this level is not clear, although in some cases the higher degree of intoxication is unintended or just "sneaks up" until they realize too late they have gone too far.

For others, the intent is to deliberately pass some safe threshold and get drunk. They want to drink as much as they can, regardless of the ultimate consequences. When addiction sets in, however, they can no longer obviously control their drinking. This situation is illustrated in the following brief description of an alcoholic male physician:

> Dr. Prescott, an eminent surgeon, had just gotten back from the liquor store with a pint of vodka, took four quick swallows, and thought, "It will be just about fifteen minutes before these damned shakes are gone." At that moment, insight struck, and he realized that he had become physically dependent on alcohol. His self-esteem was severely shaken by this shocking discovery, the awareness that he was lacking control. That was when he decided to quit drinking.[38]

When people start drinking alcohol they probably do not consider that they may be taking the first steps toward harming their health. And for most people, drinking does not lead to alcoholism. However, for those who do become alcoholics, the sense that they are taking a risk is often absent in the beginning and may even remain so until they are past the point of being able to control their intake.

Consequently, as shown in the risk response continuum model in Figure 1-1 in Chapter 1, control is the critical variable. High control works both ways. Those engaged in active acceptance of drinking (such as people who only drink socially) or active seeking of alcohol (people who enjoy the effects and taste) can use their high level of control to stop drinking when necessary. Or, conversely, their acceptance or seeking of alcohol may eventually cause them to lose control as physiological and/or psychological dependence takes over. In this situation, the person makes the transition from high to low control and enters the stage of passive acceptance or passive denial of the risk of alcohol. As long as agency (choice) is operative, drinking can be controlled, while structure either enables or constrains the risk. We know, as noted, that people in the upper-middle and upper-social classes often drink more or less routinely, especially at social occasions, while the lower class contains both the greatest proportion of those who abstain or have serious problems with drinking. In the latter circumstance, the structure of social conditions does not constrain drinking—but promotes it in a context of reduced opportunities and disadvantaged life situations.

Why do people drink? In sum, because they acquire a taste for it, like the physical sensations (the "buzz") associated with it, find it facilitates social interaction, and either do not consider the possibility that it could lead to alcoholism or rationalize the risk is remote at best. As long as they can control their intake and alcohol-related behavior, alcohol is a substance that is enjoyed by many people. But for other people, the risk is too great and they succumb to alcoholism and the problems associated with it.

Notes

1. Norman K. Denzin. 1987. *The Alcoholic Self.* Newbury Park, CA: Sage, p. 29.
2. Mark Keller. 1958. *The Alcohol Language.* Toronto: University of Toronto Press, p. 1.
3. M. H. Criqui and B. L. Ringel. 1994. "Does Diet or Alcohol Explain the French Paradox?" *Lancet*, 34: 1717–1723; David M. Goldberg. 1995. "Does Wine Work?" *Clinical Chemistry*, 41: 14–16.
4. Seldon D. Bacon (ed.). 1958. *Understanding Alcoholism.* Philadelphia: American Academy of Political and Social Sciences.
5. Carole Cain. 1991. *Ethos*, 2: 210–253.
6. Arnold M. Ludwig. 1988. *Understanding the Alcoholic's Mind.* New York: Oxford University Press, p. 80.
7. FBI. 2004. *FBI Reports.* Washington, D.C.: U.S. Government Printing Office.
8. Christine Lindquist, William C. Cockerham, and Sean-Shong Hwang. 1999. "Drinking Patterns in the American Deep South." *Journal of Studies on Alcohol,* 60: 663–666.
9. National Institute of Alcohol Abuse and Alcoholism. 2004. *U.S. Apparent Alcohol Consumption: National, State, and Regional Trends, 1977–2002,* No. 66 (August). NIAAA: Washington, D.C.
10. Ibid.
11. Ibid.
12. Paul Spicer. 2001. "Culture and Restoration of Self Among Former American Indian Drinkers." *Social Science and Medicine*, 53: 227–240.
13. National Institute on Alcohol Abuse and Alcoholism. 2002. *Alcohol Alert*, No. 55 (January). NIAAA: Washington, D.C.
14. Lindquist et al.

15. Raul Caetano, Catherine L. Clark, and Tammy Tam. 1998. "Alcohol Consumption Among Racial/Ethnic Minorities." *Alcohol Health and Research World*, 22: 233–241.

16. Ibid.

17. G. O'Connor. 1996. "Alcoholism in Irish American Catholics: Cultural Stereotype vs. Clinical Reality." *American Journal on Addictions*, 5: 124–135.

18. Caetano et al.

19. John Dollard. 1945. "Drinking Mores of the Social Classes." In *Alcohol, Science, and Society*. New Haven: Yale University, pp. 95–104.

20. Denzin, p. 94.

21. Dollard.

22. Lindquist et al.

23. Elton B. McNeil. 1967. *The Quiet Furies*. Englewood Cliffs, NJ: Prentice-Hall, p. 130.

24. E. M. Jellinck. 1960. *The Disease Concept of Alcoholism*. New Brunswick, NJ: Hillhouse Press.

25. Ludwig, p. 77.

26. Ibid., pp. 77–78.

27. Andrée Demers, Sylvia Kairouz, Edward M. Adlaf, Louis Gliksman, Brenda Newton-Taylor, and Alain Marchand. 2001. "Multilevel Analysis of Situational Drinking Among Canadian Undergraduates." *Social Science and Medicine*, 55: 415–424.

28. Andrée Demers, Jocelyn Bisson, and Jézabelle Palluy. 1999. "Wives' Convergence with Their Husbands' Alcohol Use: Social Conditions as Mediators." *Journal of Studies on Alcohol*, 60: 368–377.

29. Kathleen A. Parks, Brenda A. Miller, R. Lorraine Collins, and Lisa Zetes-Zanatta. 1998. "Women's Descriptions of Drinking in Bars: Reasons and Risks." *Sex Roles*, 38: 706.

30. Ibid.

31. Cynthia A. Robbins and Steven S. Martin. 1993. "Gender, Styles of Deviance, and Drinking Problems." *Journal of Health and Social Behavior*, 34: 317.

32. Robert F. Bales. 1946. "Cultural Differences in Rates of Alcoholism." *Quarterly Journal of Studies on Alcohol*, 6: 480–499.

33. Robert K. Merton. 1938. "Social Structure and Anomie." *American Sociological Review*, 3: 672–682.

34. Edwin M. Lemert. 1972. *Human Deviance, Social Problems, and Social Control*, 2nd ed. Englewood Cliffs, NJ: Prentice-Hall.

35. Denzin.

36. Ibid., p. 195.

37. Parks et al., p. 708.

38. Ludwig, pp. 76–77.

Illicit Drugs

This chapter examines why certain persons risk illicit or illegal drug use as part of their health lifestyle. Such drug use in the United States is not only a health risk, it is also a criminal activity. The people who use illicit drugs and the people who sell them can be arrested, incarcerated, and fined for violating the law. Yet drug use continues in the face of these sanctions and remains one of the nation's most persistent social problems. Probably no one sets out to be a drug addict, but for some people that is the outcome and this chapter explores why this occurs.

Drug Use as a Criminal Activity

Traditionally, the dominant American value system has approved of drug use only for therapeutic purposes under the supervision of a physician. This ethic concerning drugs goes beyond the notion that if all a drug does is make you feel good, that drug is bad because of the potential for physiological damage, addiction, and a host of social problems. The obvious exceptions are alcohol and tobacco, which are harmful yet legal to use by adults for pleasure. Prescription and over-the-counter (nonprescription) drugs, like painkillers, anxiety-reducing agents, sedatives, anti-allergy compounds, antidepressants, weight-control and birth-control bills, and other medications, are legal and used in vast amounts in the United States. In 2003, they constituted a $163 billion business. Other drugs like the opiates (opium, heroin, and the nonmedical use of codeine and morphine), cocaine, amphetamines, cannabis (marijuana, hashish, THC), and hallucinogens (LSD and PCP "angel dust") are defined as illicit and their purchase and use are punishable by law.

American society is a drug-using society. Millions of Americans not only turn to drugs to help them deal with the various tensions, anxieties, and discomforts they experience, but many people even use a drug, coffee, to help them begin the day. Pharmaceutical companies literally bombard the general public and health professionals with advertisements extolling the virtues of various pills, tablets, and salves to help them look or feel better and younger, or facilitate the functions of their livers, stomachs, and bowels, or enable them to relax, feel less tense, and sleep. Much of this drug-taking tendency most likely originates from the medical professional's general attitude toward drugs as "magic bullets" that can be shot into the human body to cure or control illnesses. Likewise, the general public seems to have adopted the notion that using prescription and over-the-counter drugs provides a quick and satisfactory solution to many of the physical and psychological problems of daily living.

Illicit drug use was not considered to be a major social problem in the United States until the late-nineteenth century. At that time, opium and its derivative morphine, led to the first widespread drug addiction. According to Oakley Ray, three events encouraged this development.[1] First, the hypodermic syringe was invented, making it possible for morphine to be used extensively, and sometimes not too wisely, during the American Civil War for the treatment of pain and dysentery. So many veterans were addicted to morphine after the war that it was called the "soldier's disease." Second, the smoking of opium spread rapidly after its introduction to American society by Chinese workers imported to build railroads in the West after the Civil War. Third, and most important, many widely distributed patent medicines of the day, whose manufacture were largely unregulated, contained opium as a main ingredient. Laudanum, for example, one of the most famous and potent painkillers popular in the Old West, contained one grain of opium for every twenty drops of alcohol. Many Americans, not surprisingly, were physically dependent on some form of opium or its derivatives, because of its use in patent medicines.

Public reaction to the social problems posed by opium at the beginning of the twentieth century eventually resulted in a series of legislative acts—the Food and Drug Act of 1906, the Opium Exclusion Act of 1909, the Harrison Act of 1914, among others—which attempted to control the importation and use of drugs then considered harmful. This legislation made it impossible to legally purchase controlled drugs and a large illegal market arose to meet the needs of people who wanted them. This market was fueled by the considerable profits that could be made from selling drugs illegally. Public attitudes toward illicit drug use began associating such use with criminals and criminal activity. In addition, illicit drug use came to be considered, until the 1960s, a phenomenon mostly associated with the lower classes and racial/ethnic minorities living in inner-city slums. Drug abuse and addiction were regarded as a symptom of not only crime and juvenile delinquency, but also of poverty and disadvantaged living conditions.

The belief that drug abuse and addiction were largely confined to the lower-social classes disappeared in the late 1960s with the entry of large numbers of middle-class youth into a drug-oriented "hippie" subculture. This subculture espoused an ethic of immediate self-gratification (sex and drugs) and challenged traditional views of authority, morality, and the inevitability of progress, while demanding an end to racism and the Vietnam War. Once a drug culture spread into middle- and upper-middle-class neighborhoods, public concern rapidly grew and U.S. drug laws were modernized.

The Comprehensive Drug Abuse Prevention and Control Act of 1970 repealed and replaced all prior federal laws dealing with illicit drugs. The new law shifted responsibility for enforcement from the U.S. Treasury Department to the Department of Justice. The main target of the law was the drug seller or "pusher" against whom there were severe penalties, rather than the person found in possession of a controlled drug. There were, initially, few penalties for possessing only small amounts of controlled substances. But the 1988 Omnibus Drug Act changed this situation by imposing fines, requiring the forfeiture of cars, boats, or airplanes conveying the drugs, and mandating the loss of federal benefits like student loans for simply possessing illicit drugs. Funds were also made available to support drug treatment programs. Drug dealing, use, and/or possession were now clearly defined as criminal problems in the United States.

Psychoactive Drug Action

Most sociological studies of drug use focus on drugs classified as psychoactive, in that their effects are primarily on the brain and result in changes in mood, perception, and consciousness. Psychoactive drugs affect the ability of the central nervous system to process information by altering the sensitivity of neurons. As Oakley Ray and Charles Ksir explain, the basic fact in understanding the actions of drugs is that the drug molecule forms a physiochemical bond with a neurotransmitter receptor which transmits information between neurons in the central nervous system.[2] The action of the drug either mimics, facilitates, or antagonizes a normally occurring physiochemical process, while increasing, decreasing, or disrupting a neurotransmitter's normal activity and sensitivity. The extent of the drug's effect is determined by the type of drug and the amount or dose concentrated at the site of the action. Psychoactive drugs do not cause a new form of nerve action, but they do alter the normal actions of the neurons.

Social Patterns of Drug Use

This section examines the differences in illegal drug use among different groups. However, it is impossible to know exactly how many people use these drugs and in what amounts and frequency they are consumed. Because the use of illicit drugs can result in serious social and legal penalties for the drug dealer or offender, it is logical to assume most drug use is hidden. We do have some self-reports from drug-takers, but most of what we know is based on data from law-enforcement agencies.

Age and Gender

The greatest prevalence of illicit psychoactive drug use occurs among adolescents and adults under the age of 30 years. It also appears that illicit drug use declines with age. Marijuana and cocaine use, for example, usually decrease after the mid-20s, but heroin use may continue through the 30s before declining. Some people, of course, persist in their drug habits past the point others of their age have stopped, but usually age is an important identifier of drug use. As for gender, males are more likely than females to use illicit drugs and also to begin using them at earlier ages, regardless of the type of drug. Although use by females is increasing, illicit drug use remains a predominantly male risk behavior.

Socioeconomic Status and Race

The once conventional stereotype of the illicit drug user as a lower-class resident of a slum in a large city has been transformed by the spread of drugs throughout American society, especially among teenagers and young adults in the middle class. Prior to the 1960s, marijuana was a lower-class drug, but it is now identified more with the middle and upper class. The social image of the typical marijuana user has become that of a person who is young, white, well-educated, and middle class.

For opiate addiction, especially heroin, the stereotype of the lower-class drug user still has some validity because these drugs remain concentrated among users in poor neighborhoods. Heroin addiction, unlike cocaine addiction, never became popular or "chic," although both began as lower-class drugs, possibly because heroin addiction is so powerful and, ultimately, the physical effects are so devastating to the well-being of the addict. But it would be incorrect to presume that one social class uses a particular drug and another social class generally avoids it. Use of all illicit drugs occurs throughout the class structure, even though some classes may feature greater use of some drugs than others.

The same situation exists along racial lines. Persons of every racial background use different types of illicit drugs. A nationwide sample of persons 12 years of age and over in 2002–2003 found some 12.1 percent of Native Americans and Alaskan Natives (Eskimos and other native peoples from Alaska) had used some type of illicit drug in the previous month, followed by persons of mixed races (12.0 percent) and Native Hawaiians and Pacific Islanders living in the U.S. (11.1 percent).[3] Among the major population groups, there was no significant difference in the percentages of non-Hispanic blacks (8.7 percent), non-Hispanic whites (8.3 percent), and Hispanics (8.0 percent) using illicit drugs. Asian Americans were last, with 3.8 percent having used an illicit drug in the previous month.

Regarding the use of specific drugs, marijuana is especially prevalent among American Indians/Native Alaskans and Native Hawaiians/Pacific Islanders, although its use has spread among all races. The relationship between race and class in illicit drug use is especially noteworthy among whites. While significant numbers of middle-class whites turned to heroin use in the late 1960s and early 1970s, this is no longer the case. Heroin has returned to poor neighborhoods, with today's users predominantly white males over age 30 who live in inner-city slums.[4] Middle- and upper-class whites are more likely to use marijuana and cocaine. To understand why anyone, black, white, Asian, or Hispanic would risk his or her health by using illicit drugs, we examine marijuana, heroin, and cocaine use in more detail in the next sections.

Marijuana

Marijuana is the most popular illicit drug, and its effects are relatively mild in comparison to "hard" drugs like heroin and cocaine that are highly addictive. Marijuana is composed of finely ground cannabis leaves and is usually self-administered by smoking, for example, a cigarette (a "joint"), but in concentrated form its smoke may be consumed as hashish through a water pipe or the leaf can be eaten in baked goods. The psychoactive agent is tetrahydrocannibol (THC), a potent chemical that, when smoked, quickly affects the brain by causing a release of dopamine in the forebrain. The user typically experiences a sense of well-being, relaxation, as well as enhanced physical and emotional sensitivity, including feelings of exceptional closeness to others. Other effects of being "stoned" are a distorted sense of time and problems with short-term memory. According to pharmacologist Avram Goldstein, thoughts may ramble out of control, and things may seem funny to the smoker that are not at all humorous to an observer. "The most obvious behavioral abnormality displayed by a subject under the influence of cannabis is difficulty in carrying on an intelligible conversation, perhaps because of an inability to remember what was just said."[5]

Research shows that the major reason people smoke marijuana is pleasure. Marijuana users "seek a sense of well-being (euphoria)—a relaxed, calm, drowsy, dreamlike state, with a feeling of disconnection from the ordinary world."[6] Thus, enjoyment of the mind-affecting experience is what primarily motivates people to become users. The drug is also known to facilitate social interaction because it can help people relax and is often used in the company of friends. Marijuana might be described as the most social of drugs in that its use typically begins as a result of peer influence. Past research on adolescent marijuana smokers shows them to be closely involved with their peers, as well as typically espousing a more liberal political ideology than nonusers, being less interested in school, and more likely to have tried beer and wine, distilled spirits, and cigarettes.

Becoming a Marijuana User

Sociologist Howard Becker, who conducted a major study of marijuana use among jazz musicians several years ago, found that a person had to learn to smoke marijuana.[7] Three steps were necessary to becoming a marijuana user: (1) learning the technique, (2) learning to perceive the effects, and (3) learning to enjoy the effects. Becker says that first the user must learn to develop the proper smoking techniques if the drug is to produce pleasure, and this is usually accomplished by smoking it with other people who explain how to do it. Learning the smoking technique is not enough; the person must also learn to perceive the effects as pleasurable. Becker explains:

> . . . being high consists of two elements: the presence of symptoms caused by [marijuana] use and the recognition of these symptoms and their connection

by the user with his [or her] use of the drug. It is not enough, that is, that the effects be present; alone they do not automatically provide the experience of being high. . . . The novice, then, eager to have this feeling, picks up from the other users, some concrete referents of the term "high" and applies these notions to his [or her] own experience. The new concepts make it possible for him [or her] to locate these symptoms among his or [her] own sensations and point out to himself [or herself] "something different" in his [or her] experience that he [or she] connects with drug use.[8]

Once the novice smoker has learned to get "high," Becker says that it is necessary that the person learns to enjoy the effects if the drug use is to continue. This step is required because marijuana-produced sensations are not automatically pleasurable and the taste for such an experience is "socially acquired." Many times a person's initial experience of being "high" will be confusing, fearful, or unpleasant. Becker provides the following example of an unpleasant first experience of smoking marijuana taken from one of his interviews:

> . . . I'll tell you one thing. I never did enjoy it at all. I mean it was just nothing that I could enjoy. (Well, did you get high when you turned on?) Oh, yeah, I got definite feelings from it. But I didn't enjoy them. I mean I got plenty of reactions, but they were mostly reactions of fear. (You were frightened?) Yes. . . . I couldn't seem to relax with it, you know. If you can't relax with a thing, you can't enjoy it, I don't think.[9]

So it becomes necessary for the experienced user to teach the novice to enjoy the experience. The experienced user accomplishes this by reassuring the novice about unpleasant sensations and minimizing their seriousness, while simultaneously emphasizing the pleasurable aspects. Eventually, the experienced user will not only teach the novice to enjoy the pleasurable sensations, but also to define those ambiguous sensations formerly regarded as unpleasant as actually being enjoyable. Becker concludes that a person does not become a marijuana user unless he or she has learned to smoke the drug in a way that will produce a "high," has learned to recognize the effects and connect them with marijuana, and has learned to enjoy the sensations the drug has produced. That person has, in effect, learned to answer "yes" to the question: "Is smoking marijuana fun?"

Marijuana's Effects

Considerable misinformation exists about marijuana use. Some of this misleading information likely emerged during the 1920s and 1930s from mass media "scare tactics" employed to influence legislation opposing use of the drug. One of the most common myths about marijuana that persists even today is that it is not addictive. Evidence from earlier studies that marijuana does not produce physical dependence or withdrawal symptoms possibly helped weaken claims of the drug's addictive potential. In addition, research has shown that the human body does not develop a tissue tolerance to marijuana, so the same quantity or dose consumed usually produces the same effects repeatedly, unlike in the case, for example, of alcohol or tobacco. However, recent research shows that, after heavy use of marijuana, people experience withdrawal symptoms of irritability, restlessness, loss of appetite, sleeplessness, tremors, perspiration, and occasionally nausea, vomiting, and diarrhea.[10] Many of the symptoms are behavioral, rather than physical, but occur nonetheless.

But, if overall, addiction to marijuana is rare, it does seem to occur among a small number of users who become compulsive about inhaling the drug and allowing it to dominate their lives to the exclusion of other activities.[11]

Some also claim that marijuana causes an *amotivational* syndrome, in that regular marijuana users become passive, lack ambition, and are nonproductive, but there is no evidence proving this is definitely the case. Evidence of potential physiological harm brought on by extensive marijuana use is uncertain and controversial. In rats and monkeys, high doses have produced brain damage, but similar evidence for humans is inconclusive.[12] Nevertheless, pregnant women are warned to avoid heavy use. Another problem is cancer, especially lung cancer. We do know that cannabis smoke contains more carcinogens than tobacco smoke, so heavy marijuana users are again at risk.[13]

As for sex, there is no proof that marijuana is an aphrodisiac. If marijuana does increase sexual desire, such desire is most likely psychological in that the user equates sexuality with the marijuana experience. He or she does so because that experience induces feelings of closeness with others and increases sensitivity to sensory stimuli. So increased desire may result from increased suggestibility and also perhaps from a reduction in inhibitions. But the drug alone apparently has no effect on sexual desire and may actually weaken it because marijuana tends to reduce physical drive. About the best that can be said for marijuana as a sexual stimulant is that if a person is sexually oriented, then marijuana may help by releasing inhibitions; otherwise, it has no effect.

It is clear that performance on complex tasks is adversely affected by marijuana use, and disturbances in mental functions can last for up to 24 hours or more. Goldstein reports on a test involving airline pilots and marijuana use in which a pilot, after smoking marijuana the day before, is directed in a flight simulator to land an aircraft safely on a runway without being able to see anything because of fog. To land, the pilot must depend on his flight instruments and be in constant communication with an air controller. Goldstein says:

> Before the test begins, the pilot reports he feels up to par, that he would feel comfortable flying a real airplane right now, and that he has no doubt about his ability to carry out the standard instrument landing procedure. But he is wrong. His performance is so poor that if he were flying an actual airplane there might be real danger. Yet the only thing different today is that—as part of an experiment—he had smoked a single marijuana cigarette, and that his exposure to cannabis had occurred 24 hours before.[14]

In sum, as Goldstein observes, while marijuana and hashish are not as dangerous as some addictive drugs, they impair judgment and heavy use over time may have a variety of adverse consequences. Marijuana use in the United States has declined somewhat since the 1960s and 1970s. Although still used on occasion by large numbers of adolescents and young adults, especially white middle-class youth, regular use is not as widespread. Public and peer disapproval of habitual use and greater awareness of the risks in taking the drug over time have contributed to the situation. Being a "pothead" is not a desired social role when good grades and job success are more important for ambitious youth.

Heroin

Originally developed as an analgesic and cough suppressant by the Bayer Company in Germany in 1890 and made commercially available in 1898, heroin has become the classic drug of addiction. Heroin is a laboratory-produced derivative of morphine. When injected with a syringe into a vein, heroin reaches the brain in seconds. It produces an intense feeling of sublime pleasure (a "rush"), followed by the mellow sensation of a tranquil dreamlike state in which there is an emotional disconnection with reality.[15] Heroin sold on the street was often heavily diluted in the past by other substances like sugar, but greater availability and competition has generally resulted in much less dilution. Consequently, some people, usually middle class, who would refuse intravenous injection because of its association with squalor and slum-area drug addicts, snort or smoke heroin. Overseas, smoking heroin is a particularly common form of ingestion in China, Southeast Asia, and India.[16] But addiction is possible just the same.

Goldstein interviewed several heroin addicts about their initial experiences with injecting the drug, which usually occurred in adolescence. The most apt description he was provided with was that of experiencing "an overwhelming sensation of otherworldly bliss."[17] The desire to re-create this sensation turns into a craving that is increasingly difficult to satisfy, leading to addiction. Goldstein suggests that people who risk becoming heroin addicts typically deny it will happen to them and initially try the drug out of curiosity. Usually, these are people who have experience with alcohol, cigarettes, and illicit drugs, like marijuana, so they view heroin as just another phase of substance experimentation or use. "All of them," states Goldstein, "at the time, had known perfectly well the dangers of addiction, but succumbed to curiosity (often at the urging of friends), rationalizing that although others might become addicted, they would not."[18]

Although the first use of heroin promotes nausea and vomiting, adverse reactions to these unpleasant side effects are usually overcome by the drug's pleasurable sensations. Continued use of heroin causes these side effects to lessen. Tolerance and dependence develop rapidly, so weekly use turns into wanting "a fix" every few days, to daily use, and finally to using the drug 3 to 4 times a day as addiction fully sets in. When addicts go without the drug, they feel sick, and need a shot of heroin to provide relief. As time goes by and heroin use continues, they must have increasing amounts to relieve the sickness and re-create the euphoria it originally provided.

Therefore, using heroin on a regular basis is a self-defeating process not only because of the difficult social and legal situation addicts find themselves in, but also because the pleasure derived from the drug gradually lessens over time. Eventually, addicts discover that their desire for pleasure has been replaced by a desire to avoid the pain of withdrawal. Nausea and vomiting are common reactions to the injection of heroin into the body, but chronic intoxication can produce permanent physiological difficulties, including constriction of the pupils of the eye, muscle spasms, constipation, impotence for men, and failure to menstruate for women.

Cocaine

The drug of choice for many users in the middle and upper class in recent years is cocaine. Americans consumed 259 metric tons of cocaine at a cost of $35.3 billion in 2000, a decrease from the 447 tons used and $69.9 billion spent in 1990.[19] Cocaine is a natural substance extracted from coca leaves and sold in crystal form or chopped into a white odorless powder. As a powder, cocaine is snorted and enters the nervous system through a nasal passage. It can take up to three minutes to feel the effects. The crystal form of cocaine, called "crack cocaine," cannot be dissolved by water and is smoked in a specially designed water pipe that filters and passes the smoke into the lungs, from where it reaches the brain in seconds. Crack cocaine is easily smoked, relatively cheap, and popular among people who would not consider injecting themselves in a vein with a syringe. Most of those who become addicted start out snorting cocaine on a social, recreational basis until using the drug becomes a necessity. Cocaine addiction is evident when someone shows a loss of control over taking the drug. The person cannot turn it down when offered or control the amount used.

Goldstein reports that the immediate effects of a small dose of cocaine are an extremely pleasurable sensation (a "high" or "rush") and the release of social inhibitions.[20] Talkativeness and an unrealistic sense of cleverness, heightened competence, power, and sexual prowess are common. Sexual activity may be stimulated, and Goldstein notes that the intensity of orgasms enhanced by cocaine plays a major role in the attractiveness of the drug for some users. "Extravagant sexual fantasies are common and are often acted upon, so all sorts of uninhibited and aberrant sexual behaviors may be indulged in, which the user would not ordinarily condone."[21] The effects, however, last only ten minutes or so. Goldstein describes how cocaine makes a fictitious person named "Roger Whitcomb" feel:

> Roger Whitcomb is absent from his office this afternoon. Unable to wait until evening, the craving nagging at him relentlessly, he quit work and raced home. He is missing important business, but no business is as important as what he is about to do. Sitting on a soft easy chair, he places a pellet of crack cocaine in the bowl of a little pipe. He trembles with anticipation as he lights it and inhales deeply. A few seconds later he feels it "hit." An overwhelming sense of alertness, power, deep satisfaction, almost-orgasmic pleasure sweeps over him. A few hours later, he is still at it, using up his entire $200 supply of crack cocaine, needing more and more of it to sustain the euphoria.[22]

Cocaine is destroyed in the bloodstream so rapidly that the effects of a moderate dose last, as noted, only minutes while tolerance develops rapidly. So binges with increased amounts are necessary to keep the "high" going. Goldstein reports that a cocaine binge can last up to 24 sleepless hours with several "hits" per hour, followed by a "crash" when the drug is used up. Next comes a stage of intense craving and finding more cocaine can become an obsession until another binge is initiated, or the individual manages to fight off his or her cravings. Cocaine binges can sometimes stop the heart or lead to strokes, especially if alcohol is also consumed. Distorted sensations like "bugs crawling under the skin" and paranoia can also be experienced.[23] Cocaine, like other illicit drugs, induces pleasurable feelings, but exacts a toll.

Behavorial Theories of Drug Use

Explanations of drug use caused by physiological dysfunctions inherent in certain individuals have failed to demonstrate their validity, as have similar theories attempting to explain alcoholism. A major problem with biologically based approaches to the study of drug use is that not everything is known about the biochemistry of the experience. Furthermore, some drugs, like marijuana and heroin, are social drugs because other people are required to teach the novice how to use them and interpret the experience. People cannot just try heroin, explains Goldstein, the same way they may try a new breakfast cereal bought at a supermarket.[24] First-time heroin users must have someone who is experienced show how and where to buy the drug, how to dissolve it over a flame in a spoon, filter it with cotton, put it in a syringe, tie a tourniquet to better expose a vein, insert it, and inject it. Telling the novice what to expect and explaining the sensations he or she is experiencing is also part of the training. Heroin use begins, notes Goldstein, as a "very social affair," with its own conventions and techniques.[25]

For example, Beth Crisp and her colleagues found there is often a pattern of etiquette associated with needlesharing.[26] Sharing a syringe is dangerous because of the potential for transmitting HIV or hepatitis. The person who owns the needle usually uses it first, before passing it to someone else. Or the individual who supplies the money for the drug, makes the effort to obtain it, or provides the place for injecting it, may want to use the needle before others. Or, depending on the people present, the most assertive or dominant person may insist on injecting first. Sometimes those who are thought to be free of HIV or hepatitis go first, and those who are infected inject last. It seems to be generally understood that anyone who is known to be HIV-positive would usually use the syringe last if only one syringe is available. As a respondent in the Crisp study reported:

> . . . well, my sister was with a person who was HIV positive, and he told them, he said, they had to use the same syringe. He said, "I'll use it after you because I'm HIV positive," which was very good I thought, you know, because some people wouldn't tell you, they'd try and sneak their way in. . . .[27]

The decision to risk heroin addiction is thus not an isolated singular experience involving only the psychology of one person. It is a social experience requiring interaction with others in the beginning and then being influenced by that interaction. This interaction continues while acquiring the drug and sometimes while using it. We next consider the major sociological theories that attempt to explain illicit drug use.

The Structural-Functionalist Explanation

The structural-functionalist approach, derived from the work of sociologists Emile Durkheim, Robert Merton, Talcott Parsons, and others, is based on the assumption that certain social conditions tend to produce deviance (in this case, drug addiction), regardless of the personalities of individual persons. Structural-functionalism, or simply functionalism, does not locate the causes of deviant behavior in individual needs, drives, instincts, genetic combinations, or any other purely individual variables. It identifies the source of deviant behavior as in the relationships between individuals and social systems. This approach is based on the view that society is held together in a state of equilibrium by consensual patterns of shared norms and values. What makes social life possible is the expectation that people will behave in accord with the norms and values common to their social system. This process is "functional" because it results in social harmony and counterbalances "dysfunctional" processes like crime and drug addiction that disrupt the social order.

Proponents of functionalism argue that drug addiction is concentrated in the lower class because members of this stratum experience the greatest amounts of socioeconomic deprivation. Examples of functionalist-oriented studies include those that examine the spatial distribution of heroin use and locate its concentration in the most crowded and dilapidated neighborhoods of large cities like New York City, Chicago, and Los Angeles. While certain attitudes, values, and personality characteristics may be critical in using heroin, the principal cause of addiction is usually identified as the influence of depressing living conditions. This influence is considered so pervasive that it produces a sense of hopelessness and futility that makes heroin use attractive.

Another example of the functionalist perspective on heroin addiction is the "double-failure" hypothesis presented several years ago by Richard Cloward and Lloyd Ohlin.[28] They argued that the "retreatist" mode of adaptation in Robert Merton's goals-means paradigm of social structure and anomie was not an adequate theoretical explanation of heroin addiction. As discussed in Chapter 3, a retreatist rejects both society's goals and the approved means of reaching them by dropping out of conventional society and retreating from it by becoming a solitary drug addict, tramp, or homeless person. A weakness of the retreatist argument for Cloward and Ohlin is that heroin addicts have to interact with other people. They must purchase the drug, acquire the money to pay for it, and may use it in settings with other people. So while heroin addicts may retreat from mainstream society, they cannot retreat into complete isolation from other people because they need others to support their drug habit.

The double-failure hypothesis is based upon the idea that lower-class adolescent drug users have internalized society's goals about striving toward success, but have failed to achieve those goals in both legitimate and illegitimate ways. Thus, heroin users turn to the drug because of a double failure in both the conventional and criminal world. When heroin is used as a solution to being a "failure," that person's social relationships will obviously be adversely affected. Habitual drug use is not a valued activity even among juvenile gangs. Drug addicts are viewed as weak by the strong. Therefore, Cloward and Ohlin suggest that the heroin user does indeed "retreat," but does so in isolation from his or her peer group, relying on the drug as a solution to status deprivation.

While some sociologists regard the Cloward and Ohlin double-failure hypothesis as either a theory of lower-class adolescent drug use or as a general theory of addiction, it is neither. The theory fails to explain why some persons similarly situated in the lower class use drugs while others do not. All lower-class heroin users may not be double failures. People can also be double failures, yet not turn to heroin. But the major difficulty with the theory involves Cloward and Ohlin's attempt to maintain that the heroin addict is a retreatist. Despite their recognition that drug addiction requires very active, nonretreatist behavior, Cloward and Ohlin insist that the failure to reach the goals of either the legitimate or illegitimate social worlds cause people who are double failures to be vulnerable to retreatist behavior. Their retreatism will be facilitated by drug addiction.

Yet it is clear that addicts must attach great significance to monetary situations to pay for their habit. Taking drugs becomes increasingly expensive since greater quantities are needed over time, and drug dealers often increase prices for addicts to make larger profits. Users must therefore find the financial means to support their addiction. Unless they are independently wealthy, they must either have a job or turn to criminal activities like drug dealing, theft, robbery, and prostitution. These behaviors put them in active contact with some people on a regular basis. While heroin addicts do retreat from conventional social life, they are active in the world of the addicted, and this activity undermines the notion of their retreatism.

While retreatism is not the optimal explanation of drug addiction, the functionalist perspective nevertheless contributes to our understanding of why people risk becoming addicted to drugs. The basis for this statement is derived from Durkheim's work on suicide.[29] Durkheim suggested that suicide, despite its highly personal nature, is not entirely an act of free choice by the individual. He based this conclusion on his observation that the suicide rates for various Western European countries were relatively constant year after year. That is, about the same percentage of people killed themselves annually in each country. Therefore, something more than simply individual motives and circumstances appeared to be involved. "Wholly different," states Durkheim, "are the results we obtained when we forgot the individual and sought the causes of the suicidal aptitude of each society in the nature of the societies themselves."[30] It was the individual's relationship to the larger social order and the manner in which this relationship was altered that provided the catalyst for suicide. The key insight in Durkheim's theory that informs our understanding of drug addiction is that societal-level processes and conditions can create stressful circumstances whereby people are forced to respond to the situations in which they find themselves. Taking drugs can be one response to living in an adverse social environment.

Differential Association Theory

Another view of the causes of drug addiction comes from differential association theory. The basic message of this theory is that people learn to use drugs because they have spent time in the company of users who teach them the methods for using drugs. We have already seen in this chapter that the techniques for smoking marijuana and injecting heroin are learned from other people, and other people are also needed to be on hand at the time to interpret for novice users what is happening to them. Edwin Sutherland introduced the concept of differential association by maintaining that everyone goes through a process of socialization, regardless of whether he or she is learning to conform to society's norms and values, or being taught to be deviant.[31] Therefore, it is through interaction with other people that people learn deviant behavior and law-breaking. They also learn the attitudes, excuses, and definitions of the situation that these others use to justify their own deviant activities.

Differential association theory is a theoretical concept of what happens when a person falls in with "bad company." These peers teach the novice to take drugs or do other things that are against the law. People who have the most exposure to circumstances in which violating the law is permissible, says Sutherland, are the most likely to become criminals or other types who commit criminal acts such as drug users, pimps, and prostitutes. People who commit criminal acts do so because they have learned from others that these behaviors can be rewarding. But although it offers some valuable insights, differential association theory is not a complete theory of deviant behavior (e.g., heroin use) because not everybody who learns deviant acts commits them and deviance can be influenced by factors (e.g., adverse socioeconomic circumstances, opportunity) that have little or nothing to do with learning.

Labeling Theory

Labeling theory evolved out of symbolic interaction theory in sociology. According to labeling theory, once a person is defined, or labeled, by other people in a certain way, the others will respond to him or her in accordance with the label. Labeling theory is not really a theory at all; it is what Herbert Blumer called a sensitizing concept.[32] It is sensitizing in that it is intended to provide a general sense of reference and suggest directions for future research; it is not intended as a definitive statement. Nevertheless, labeling theory has emerged as a major sociological approach to understanding deviance, including drug addiction. The foundations for labeling theory come principally from the work of two American sociologists, Edwin Lemert and Howard Becker.

Lemert argues that studies of deviant behavior must confront two problems: (1) how deviant behavior originates, and (2) how deviant acts become symbolically attached to certain persons and what the consequences of such attachment then are for those individuals.[33] He believes that functionalist theory had particularly failed to address itself to the latter.

To do this, Lemert came up with the concept of *primary* and *secondary deviance*. Primary deviance is a situation in which a person does something deviant, but the behavior is rationalized as atypical by others, since it is perceived to be uncharacteristic of the person performing it. Secondary deviance is more serious because it is a situation in which a person is labeled deviant because his or her behavior is thought to be typical for that individual. Secondary deviance occurs when a person continues over time to violate norms (e.g., take drugs) and is subsequently forced by the reactions of other people to assume the social identity of a deviant (e.g., a drug user). For example, drug use may be regarded initially as primary deviance, but a heavy drug user may be relegated to a position of secondary deviance by others who define him or her as a drug addict. The person may then find it necessary to locate a group that will accommodate the deviance. The result may be that the person is forced to develop associations with other people who sell and/or take drugs and accept drug use as normal for them. Addicts are thus set apart from nonusers by society and often develop a way of life that has drug-taking at its center.

Becker made additional contributions to labeling theory in his book *Outsiders*.[34] In it he argues that social groups create deviance (here, smoking marijuana) by making rules whose infraction constitutes deviance. *Deviance is therefore not a quality of the act a person commits but rather is a consequence of the definition applied to the act by others.* Whether an act is deviant thus depends on how other people react to it. However, the responses of other people are problematic, since their interpretation of the situation is the deciding factor, and not all people see things the same way. The focus of *Outsiders* is on habitual marijuana smokers who view marijuana use as normative behavior in their own subculture but who are lawbreakers in the view of the wider society.

Other factors may be significant in responses to deviance. Becker states, for instance, that responses to a particular act may vary over time; if there is a police crackdown on gambling, responses to gambling may be harsher than at other times. However, when it comes to drugs, especially drug dealing, responses are typically harsh by the criminal justice system. Responses to deviant behavior also depend on who commits the act and who feels harmed by it. Rules are sometimes more likely to be enforced with some people than others. For example, a lower-class delinquent male may be more likely to be arrested, convicted, and sentenced than an upper-class delinquent male who commits the same offense.

Becker maintains that some behavior is classified as obedient to rules and other behavior as rule breaking, yet whether a particular individual is defined as deviant depends on the perceptions of others. Conformists are people who are not perceived as deviant and are not in fact deviant; the falsely accused are people who are perceived as deviant but in fact are innocent. In describing people who are actually rule breakers, there are two types: the pure deviant who is both deviant and perceived as such, and the secret deviant who is deviant but not perceived as such. An example of a secret deviant is someone who snorts cocaine only when alone and in the privacy of his or her home, and is careful to conceal this activity from others.

Labeling theory emphasizes that judgments about what constitutes deviance in a person are relative, depending on the perceptions of other people. The critical variable in understanding deviant behavior is the social audience that has knowledge of the act in question, since the audience determines what is and what is not deviance.

Despite its value in providing a strategy for analyzing the range of perceptions people may hold about deviant acts and deviant persons, labeling theory has some serious weaknesses. Lemert's concentration on the transition from primary to secondary deviance neglects the question of what initially caused the deviance. This criticism can be applied to labeling theory as a whole, because societal reaction alone fails to explain why certain people commit deviant acts while others in the same circumstances do not. A label in itself does not cause deviance. Drug addiction, alcoholism, suicide, and crime are generally defined by society as deviant—yet people engage in these behaviors regardless of how they are labeled, and their reasons may have nothing to do with the label that is attached to them.

Another problem is Becker's notion of the secret deviant. If a deviant status is determined by the reaction of the social audience, how can a secret deviant be labeled as "deviant" if no one knows about his or her behavior? Becker attempts to refute this criticism by claiming that secret deviance involves being vulnerable to discovery, that is, of being in a position in which it would be easy to make a deviant label stick. In such a circumstance, secret deviants know they will be labeled deviant if discovered. But this explanation also does not tell us how or why the deviance began.

Another deficiency of labeling theory is that it does not account for the characteristics of deviants or deviant acts. Deviant behavior is often an action initiated by people to cope with problems brought on by a social situation over which they have little control. Other people may have similar problems and react in a similar manner. Thus, there could be a common "cause" for their deviance, but also the acts and the people committing them may share certain other similarities (e.g., poverty, stress, age, family background). In other cases, some people may have control over their circumstances, yet opt for being deviant for a variety of reasons (e.g., self-punishment, thrills, personal gain). Again, there may be some sharing of characteristics between deviant acts and deviant people, and these characteristics may be as critical, if not more critical, than the reaction of the social audience. If the question is whether deviance is caused exclusively by societal reactions, the best answer seems to be that it cannot be.

Labeling theorists also maintain that individual behavior is not automatically determined by social situations and structures, but is derived from how people define their situation and act on the basis of that definition. Virtually all sociologists, however, would agree that human social behavior is not automatically determined in an unthinking, robotlike fashion by situations and structures. Rather, structure sometimes propels people along one path rather than another they might take because the ones they choose seem appropriate under the circumstances. But people can still have options to choose (the exercise of agency) the direction of their behavior and can act contrary to norms—which is what deviant behavior is all about. Thus, the effects of structure on behavior do not seem as heavy-handed as labeling theorists insist.

Once a person is labeled deviant, labeling theorists seem to place the labeled individual in circumstances in which that person has little or no choice about what happens. That is, once labeled, the deviant person is forced to assume a deviant status in society because that is how he or she is perceived and treated by others. Although it may seem to be a contradiction to assert that initially people have a choice about being deviant and later (once they are labeled) they do not, one strength of labeling theory lies in its recognition of the transition from primary to secondary deviance. Sometimes people do not have choices in how they are treated by others, regardless of their intentions. Ronald Akers offers the best summary of this:

> Rather, although those of this school [labeling theory] come dangerously close to saying that the actual behavior is unimportant, their contribution to the study of deviancy comes precisely in their conception of the impact of labeling on behavior. One sometimes gets the impression from reading this literature that people go about minding their own business and then— "wham"—bad society comes along and slaps them with a stigmatized label. Forced into the role of deviant, the individual has little choice but to be deviant. This is an exaggeration, of course, but such an image can be gained easily from an overemphasis on the impact of labeling. However, it is exactly this image, toned down and made reasonable, which is the central contribution of the labeling school to the sociology of deviance.[35]

Becker agrees that one of the most central contributions of labeling theory is that it focuses attention on how labeling places people in circumstances that make it difficult to continue acting as if their behavior is normal and follows the routines of everyday life. Rather than successfully resist the label applied to them, they are excluded from the company of normals by being labeled as someone whose behavior or character is offensive or unsavory. Becker contends that his intention is not to explain the cause of deviance, but to enlarge the understanding of deviant behavior by implicating the role of people other than the allegedly deviant person. For example, it would be foolish to propose that stickup men rob people simply because someone has labeled them stickup men.[36] But labels can have a powerful effect on how people are perceived and treated, and labeling theory helps us to understand this aspect of social interaction. For example, labeling theory shows that drug users by themselves are not the whole story. The reactions of law enforcement agencies, the courts, the medical profession, families, and society at large help create the social world of users and addicts as people who are set apart from others by public definition.

Recovering from Drug Use

A popular image of drug addicts is that they continue to use drugs until they become destitute and eventually die from the long-term effects of the substance or from an overdose. James McIntosh and Neil McKeganey point out this stereotype could hardly be further from the truth and that many addicts ultimately recover.[37] The two researchers studied the process of recovery among a sample of former drug addicts, several of whom had been hooked on heroin, to record these people's experience. They note that often addicts "mature out" of their addictions; that is, they reach an age—usually in their 30s—when being an addict can no longer be tolerated, so they stop using drugs and begin living a drug-free life even though the withdrawal process is difficult.

McIntosh and McKeganey found that a critical step in the recovery process was the construction of a "nonaddict" personal identity. Former addicts accomplished this by (1) reinterpreting their previous drug-using lifestyle, (2) reconstructing their sense of self, and (3) providing convincing explanations for their recovery. The reinterpretation of their former drug lifestyle consisted of accounts of seeing the drug-using world as what it was—filled with users and dealers, being addicted, feeling sick, not being respected, and the like. Eventually, in such a world addicts find themselves taking drugs not to get high, but simply to feel normal. As one male former addict reported:

> At first it was great, oh it was marvelous. When you first start taking them you're on top of the world, nothing can be bad; everything is great to you, shiny, happy, people. Then it gets the better of you and you don't even get a buzz out of it after a while. Basically you're just taking it to feel normal and that's no use. . . .
> So I'm saying to myself what's the point in this.[38]

Another female former addict recalled:

> I was really sick of life revolving around drugs and sick of the things I would do to get drugs and just sick of the drugs being the main thing in my life. Drugs came before anything, they came before myself, the house, my family. I hated the folks I was associating with and the lifestyle. But I would still do it because I was getting the drugs. I hated the lying, the cheating, the sleeping with folk I didn't like just because they had drugs on them. I just hated having no self-respect. I really hated myself, I really hated the junkie and I hated having to use my body to get drugs.[39]

These negative judgments of themselves by former addicts turned out to be important in helping them give up addiction. Not only did these individuals view their addict life as ultimately miserable, but also they saw themselves as wanting to be separated from being a junkie. Thus, they began reconstructing their sense of self by rejecting their former drug-using identity. Part of their new identity was formed through the development of a convincing explanation for their recovery. This often took the form of an unpleasant event such as death of a friend from an overdose, degradation, jail sentence, or "hitting rock bottom" in their life situation, or sometimes something positive like having a child, falling in love with a nonaddict, or getting a job. Whatever the event, successful former addicts quit using drugs, separated themselves from their drug identity, and started developing a new sense of themselves in which they were drug free.

Conclusion

Illicit drug use is a risk behavior dominated by males. Use typically begins in adolescence or early adulthood and declines with age. Among the largest racial groups, between 8 to 9 percent of all non-Hispanic blacks and whites, and Hispanics report having used an illicit drug within the previous month. Class is an important variable among whites regarding the type of drug consumed: middle- and upper-class whites favor marijuana and cocaine, while heroin use is more prevalent among the white-lower class. Marijuana is the most popular illicit drug for all races and social classes.

Returning to the risk response model shown in Figure 1-1 in Chapter 1, drug users are represented in each of the four categories of *passive denial*, *passive acceptance*, *active acceptance*, and *active seeking*. Why would someone with high control and high agency over his or her risk response actively seek out drugs and gamble with drug addiction? The reason is the pleasurable sensations the person experiences. The "high" is the primary motivating factor. This is true even though the initial experience with drugs like marijuana and heroin is often unpleasant. An experienced user is necessary to explain the effects and define which sensations are positive for the novice. Coaching is therefore an essential part of learning to enjoy drugs in the beginning. Heroin, however, is known as a drug whose pleasurable effects are not overwhelming until addiction sets in, and then the pleasure allegedly may be intense. But without heroin, the addict feels sick and needs the drug to eliminate the feeling. Consequently, pleasure and nausea operate in tandem to promote heroin use.

Pleasure is the primary catalyst for taking drugs; otherwise use would not likely be continued to the point where addiction sets in. Active seekers of drugs seek the pleasure as well as those in the state of active acceptance who realize they could become addicted, but accept the risk. Once self-control is lost, the person is an addict and is either in a state of passive acceptance (the realization that one is an addict and can do nothing about it) or passive denial (the realization that one is an addict and is powerless to stop).

However, the initial decision to take the drug in the absence of any personal experience with its pleasures, suggests other factors in using it are important as well. A key social factor is being around people who use drugs. Being in an environment of drug-taking promotes drug-taking since substances are available and use is permissible. Other factors appear to be curiosity and denial. People risk addiction because they are curious about a drug's effects and deny to themselves they will become addicts. One might say that addiction just sort of sneaks up on you. This process is evident in the following account by a heroin addict, a woman:

> You don't wake up one morning and decide to be a drug addict. . . . You become a narcotics addict because you do not have strong motivations in any other direction. Junk [heroin] wins by default. I tried it as a matter of curiosity. I drifted along taking shots when I could score. I ended up hooked. . . . You don't decide to be an addict. One morning you wake up sick and you're an addict.[40]

Whereas the denial may be a psychological rationalization, curiosity is typically a social phenomenon since most entry into drug use is facilitated by social interaction. Other people are necessary to the experience. Not only does the drug have to be obtained from someone, but also its use, as previously discussed, must be learned from others—as does the interpretation of the experience. Other people are also the source of curiosity about the drug because for novices use occurs in gatherings of drug users who introduce the substance and talk about it, thereby sparking the curiosity. As one female heroin addict described:

> I just felt that I used like everyone else did. . . . Everyone I knew ended up in the same condition. So the people I had hung out with were, what I thought, normal, for our time. . . . The ones that I always found that I was the most at ease with were the ones who done heroin.[41]

Another drug user, a young man, provides a similar account. He recalled his introduction to drugs:

> . . . it wasn't peer pressure . . . it wasn't verbal peer pressure as much as there was a group there and there was I and I hadn't tried it and they had and so they'd tried something I hadn't and I was sort of pissed off about this and I went up sort of thought oh yeah I'll give this a go and see what it's like so I did.[42]

An account by a female heroin addict shows that she became addicted because she just wanted to have fun and be wild and crazy. She started dating guys in a rock band who liked to shoot heroin. "And I just fell right into it," she says, "because I already loved the drugs."[43] Soon thereafter she was addicted. To be hooked or addicted to a drug also means having an experience that is life changing. The addict adopts new perceptions and attitudes about drugs, as well as new knowledge about his or her body and the effects of drugs within it. To the extent, however, that people risk addiction as a life changing experience in advance of that experience is unknown. The likely motivation for accepting the risk is curiosity reinforced by denial that one will become "hooked." Pleasure-seeking continues the use and once addiction is acquired, use becomes an obsession despite other intentions. Addiction pushes the individual along a downward physical, psychological, and social spiral that continues until painful and unpleasant efforts at withdrawal are permanently successful, the drug use and problems associated with it continues indefinitely, or death through misuse occurs.

Notes

1. Oakley Ray. 1972. *Drugs, Society, & Human Behavior*. St. Louis: Mosby.
2. Oakley Ray and Charles Ksir. 1990. Drugs, Society, & Human Behavior. St. Louis: Times/Mirror/Mosby.
3. National Center for Health Statistics. 2004. *Health, United States, 2004.* Washington, D.C.: U.S. Government Printing Office.
4. Office of National Drug Control Policy. 2003. *Heroin*. Rockville, MD: Drug Policy Information Clearinghouse.
5. Ray and Ksir, p. 198.
6. Ibid.
7. Howard S. Becker. 1973. *Outsiders: Studies in the Sociology of Deviance*, 2nd ed. New York: Free Press.
8. Ibid., pp. 49–50.
9. Ibid., p. 54.
10. Avram Goldstein. 2001. *Addiction: From Biology to Drug Policy*. Oxford, UK: Oxford University Press, p. 202.
11. Ibid.
12. Ibid., p. 201.
13. Ibid.
14. Ibid., pp. 195–196.
15. Ibid., p. 161.

16. John Strang, Paul Griffiths, and Michael Gossop. 1997. "Heroin Smoking by 'Chasing the Dragon': Origins and History." *Addiction*, 92: 673–683.
17. Goldstein, p. 160.
18. Ibid.
19. Office of National Drug Control Policy. 2003. *Cocaine*. Rockville, MD: Drug Policy Information Clearinghouse.
20. Goldstein, p. 182.
21. Ibid.
22. Ibid., p. 19.
23. Ibid., p. 183.
24. Ibid., p. 160.
25. Ibid.
26. Beth R. Crisp, James G. Barber, and Robyn Gilbertson. 1997. "The Etiquette of Needlesharing." *Contemporary Drug Problems*, 24: 273–291.
27. Ibid., p. 279.
28. Richard Cloward and Lloyd Ohlin. 1960. *Delinquency and Opportunity*. New York: Free Press.
29. Emile Durkheim. 1951. *Suicide*. New York: Free Press.
30. Ibid., p. 299.
31. Edwin H. Sutherland. 1939. *Principles of Criminology*, 3rd ed. Philadelphia: Lippincott.
32. Herbert Blumer. 1969. *Symbolic Interactionism*. Englewood Cliffs, NJ: Prentice-Hall.
33. Edwin M. Lemert. 1972. *Human Deviance, Social Problems, and Social Control*, 2nd ed. Englewood Cliffs, NJ: Prentice-Hall.
34. Becker.
35. Ronald L. Akers. 1967. "Problems in the Sociology of Deviance: Social Definitions and Behavior." *Social Forces*, 46: 463.
36. Becker, p. 179.
37. James McIntosh and Neil McKeganey. 2000. "Addicts' Narratives of Recovery from Drug Use: Constructing a Non-Addict Identity." *Social Science and Medicine*, 50: 1501–1510.
38. Ibid., p. 1504.
39. Ibid., p. 1505.
40. M. Rosenbaum. 1981. *Women on Heroin*. New Brunswick, NJ: Rutgers University Press.
41. Jennifer Friedman and Marisa Alicea. 1995. "Women and Heroin: The Path of Least Resistance." *Gender and Society*, 9: 438–439.
42. Elizabeth Plumridge and Jane Chetwynd. 1999. "Identity and the Social Construction of Risk: Injecting Drug Use." *Sociology of Health and Illness*, 21: 329–343.
43. Ibid., p. 438.

Smoking

It is common knowledge that smoking tobacco in the form of cigarettes, cigars, and in pipes, or chewing it, is bad for your health. Strong evidence links smoking to the risk of heart disease, atherosclerosis, stroke, lung and other cancers, emphysema and other respiratory diseases, liver disease, as well as several other health problems, thereby making it the lifestyle practice with the largest number of negative consequences for health.[1] Chewing tobacco is also unsafe because carcinogenic material in the leaves is absorbed directly in the mouth and throat and can cause cancer. In the United States, smoking causes a man to lose 13 years of life on average and a woman 14.5 years.[2] Some 440,000 people die each year from smoking-related causes.

Although the proportion of smokers in the United States has substantially declined since awareness of its effects on the body became generally known, some people still choose to smoke—with the decision to smoke or to not smoke an exercise of agency. That is, the decision to smoke is a choice. But is that choice independent of structure? The answer is no. Structure intervenes in this decision, as shown in the distinct differences between specific population groups, suggesting that decisions about smoking are not entirely an individual matter. Social structural factors like gender and social class strongly influence such decisions. For example, men are more likely than women to smoke, but they are also more likely to quit. People in the higher-social strata are highly unlikely to smoke, while among persons in the lowest levels of society smoking is more common.

The Effects of Nicotine

Nicotine is the addictive property found in tobacco leaves. Cigar and pipe smokers do not generally inhale, but nicotine is absorbed in the mouth, from where it reaches the brain via the circulatory system. In contrast, cigarette smokers usually do inhale and deeply, so nicotine directly enters their lungs. Since all the blood in the body passes through the lungs and enters the left side of the heart, from where some of it is carried to the brain, the nicotine picked up in the lungs is carried with it. The effect on the brain is pleasurable, providing instant gratification, with the nicotine experienced as a pleasant "spike." Each new inhalation repeats the sensation and reinforces the smoking behavior.[3] The smoker can regulate the rate of drug intake by the extent to which it is inhaled and the frequency of puffs. If the smoker feels dizzy or nauseated, he or she can stop or inhale less frequently, thus the smoker can control the effects of the drug.

Nicotine disappears in the body after a few hours. Nicotine levels in the blood are especially low in the morning on awakening, but increase during the day through continued smoking—only to drop again during sleep. By morning, the person who is addicted to nicotine is in withdrawal and so in intense need of smoking. This is why cigarette smokers often reach for a cigarette soon after awakening. The initial cigarette of the day invariably provides a great deal of pleasure: it gives the smoker an initial "nicotine rush" after a night's sleep.[4] Once the smoke is inhaled, feelings of discomfort from nicotine withdrawal dissipate.

Nicotine does not cause a gross impairment in behavior and can be used regularly without affecting a person's usual activities. Adults can legally purchase nicotine products and freely consume them in places where tobacco use is not prohibited. Despite increasingly higher costs, cigarettes are readily available and their costs remain affordable for many. Moreover, cigarette use is promoted through advertising in which smokers—depending on the audience—are depicted as attractive and adventuresome or sophisticated.

Several studies show that the major reason people smoke is the psychoactive effects of nicotine.[5] What are these effects? As Avram Goldstein reports: "Nicotine alleviates stress and anxiety, reduces frustration, anger, and aggressive feelings, and promotes a pleasurable state of relaxation."[6] Some people show improved attention and ability to concentrate when smoking, but it is not known if this is due to the direct effects of nicotine or nicotine's capacity to reduce stress, which could improve the smoker's ability to focus on the task at hand. From a behavioral perspective, addiction to nicotine is not dangerous to the individual or society. But it is highly dangerous to the smoker's own health. As noted, smoking has the largest number of adverse health consequences of any lifestyle practice.

For example, the major cause of lung cancer is smoking. People with lung cancer are increasingly less able to breathe adequately and feel suffocated as their lungs lose the capacity to transfer oxygen into the blood. Fatal complications are the result.[7] The physiological damage caused by smoking is not due to the ingestion of nicotine, but to the irritant and carcinogenic material ("tar") released by burning tobacco into the smoke that is inhaled. This is why secondhand smoke in the workplace or at home can be dangerous. Smokers affect the quality of air shared by other people in enclosed locations like homes, offices, automobiles, bars, and restaurants. Nonsmokers exposed to secondhand smoke or passive smoking have been shown to exhibit detectable evidence of nicotine in their lungs.[8] For example, the children of parents who smoke have significantly higher rates of breathing disorders than children whose parents do not smoke.[9] The harmful health effects of passive smoking influenced Ireland in 2004 to ban smoking from pubs and San Francisco, California, in 2005 to ban it from bars in that city. These measures were primarily intended to protect the lungs of nonsmokers who worked in bars or were customers.

While the number of people who die annually from lung cancer caused by smoking is about 200,000 in the United States, smoking accounts for another 200,000 deaths through its effects on the cardiovascular system. Smoking promotes heart attacks and strokes, narrows and hardens arteries, damages blood vessels and causes them to rupture (aneurysms), and causes high blood pressure. Smoking can be a death sentence. About one of every two people who smoke die from its effects, unless they quit.[10] Quitting smoking, even past the age of 50, tends to increase longevity, but the death toll from smoking continues to rise each year.

Social Patterns of Smoking

Age and Gender

For most smokers, smoking begins in adolescence. Adult smokers have invariably tried cigarettes by the age of 18 years, with early smokers beginning as young as 11 and 12 years.[11] Prior to the twentieth century, smoking tobacco was almost exclusively a masculine practice. Norms regarding gender and smoking at this time were clear: it was socially acceptable for men, but not for women to smoke. Gentlemen were not even supposed to smoke when in the company of ladies. As Diana Chapman Walsh and her colleagues conclude, "gender was the decisive axis dividing smokers and nonsmokers."[12] The few women who smoked were generally considered to be rebellious, or of loose morals and easy virtue. Smoking by a woman signaled her sexual availability to men. In fact, if a woman allowed a man to smoke in her presence, she was considered "fast" or unrespectable. Walsh and her colleagues argue that the widespread condemnation of smoking by women was part of a male-dominated system of social control enforced by strict rules and norms concerning gender-appropriate behavior. "Respectable" women did not smoke, because to do so was socially unacceptable and condemned when it occurred. So cigarettes were smoked by a few upper-class women who were independent enough to ignore any social sanctions or by much larger numbers of powerless lower-class women who had no social reputations to protect.[13] While the extent to which the general social prohibition against female smoking can be characterized as an expression of male repression may be debatable, the outcome was nevertheless beneficial for women because tobacco-induced diseases like lung cancer were significantly less prevalent among females.

This situation changed during World War II when women entered the civilian labor force in large numbers as replacements for men in the military. Empowered by the greater equality and independence that resulted from employment outside the home, women increased dramatically their smoking in the 1940s.[14] However, the feminine embrace of smoking was limited to cigarettes, as social norms against women smoking cigars and pipes remained. While the proportion of women smokers was never as large as that of men, their pattern of use was similar with respect to the age at which they began smoking (adolescence) and the number and types of cigarettes consumed. Female rates of lung cancer rose, accordingly, from 5.8 deaths per 100,000 in 1950 to 40.9 in 2001. Lung cancer ranked eighth among cancer deaths for women in 1961, but moved up to first by 1986, where it remains today. Deaths from lung cancer now account for 25 percent of all cancer deaths among women. This rise is attributed to an aging of female cohorts with a higher prevalence of cigarette smoking.

One reason for smoking that is more applicable to females than males is the use of cigarettes to maintain a slim body. In many societies, a slim figure symbolizes attractiveness, youth, and beauty. This image is particularly imposed by these societies through the mass media and the beauty preferences of males for slim teenage and adult females. Some females, in response, turn to cigarettes when they feel hungry to curb their appetite or take their mind off eating. They may skip meals and smoke instead, or eat only a few bites of food and then light up a cigarette. Either way, the goal is to reduce caloric intake and the potential for weight gain and thus appear trim and sexually attractive.

In response to the mounting scientific evidence that smoking is harmful, tobacco use in the United States is significantly decreasing for both sexes—but especially for men. As shown in Table 5-1, the proportion of men who smoke declined from 51.2 percent in 1965 to 24.7 percent in

Table 5-1

Percentage of Current Cigarette Smokers by Sex and Race, United States (Selected Years, 1965–2002)*.

	1965	1979	1983	1987	1993	1995	2002
Male	51.6	37.2	34.7	31.0	27.5	26.7	24.8
White	50.8	36.5	34.1	30.4	27.0	26.4	25.0
Black	59.2	44.1	41.3	39.0	33.2	28.5	26.7
Female	34.0	30.3	29.9	26.7	22.7	22.8	20.1
White	34.3	30.6	30.1	27.2	23.7	23.6	21.1
Black	32.1	30.8	31.8	27.2	19.8	22.8	18.3

*18 years of age and over, age-adjusted.
Source: National Center for Health Statistics, 2004

2001. The percentage of smokers among both white and black males decreased during this period, with the percentage of white male smokers declining from 50.4 percent to 24.9 percent and that of black male smokers falling from 58.8 percent to 27.6 percent. Table 5-1 shows that the proportion of women smoking also dropped from 33.7 percent in 1965 to 20.8 percent in 2001. Although smoking by males began declining in the 1970s, the percentage of female smokers did not significantly decrease until the late 1980s, and it has decreased overall much more slowly than that of males. In fact, Table 5-1 shows that between 1993 and 1995, smoking for women rose slightly from 22.7 percent to 22.8 percent. This increase was due to greater smoking among young women, especially young black women who are largely responsible for the rise in smoking among black females from 19.8 percent in 1993 to 22.8 percent in 1995. However, between 1995 and 2001, Table 5-1 shows that the percentage of black female smokers dropped to 17.9 percent. Meanwhile, the percentage of smokers among white females decreased steadily over the years, but remains higher than that of black females, with some 22.1 percent of white women smoking in 2001. Overall, smoking cessation has obviously been more pronounced among men than women. When gender and race are compared, black men are more likely to smoke than white men are, but white women are more likely to smoke than black women are.

Social Class

As noted in the introduction, persons with high social status are significantly less likely to smoke than those with low status. Education is a major factor in this pattern, with higher-educated people exceedingly less likely to smoke than those from lower-educational levels. For example, in the United States, adults with less than a high school education are three times as likely to smoke as individuals with a bachelor's or higher university degree.[15] A similar situation exists in Great Britain, where Andrew Adonis and Stephan Pollard point out that smoking is largely a habit of the poor.[16] They found a clear and direct relationship between smoking and social class, with rates of smoking greatest among the people at the bottom of the social ladder.

Not only do people in the lower-social strata smoke significantly more cigarettes, but they are also less likely to quit than people in the higher strata. Rates of smoking therefore combine with rates of quitting to place the heaviest risk of death from smoking-related causes on the poor. Why do the poor smoke? Martin Jarvis and Jane Wardle believe that the addictive characteristics of nicotine have much to do with it, but this does not answer why the poor are particularly drawn to smoking and are least likely to give it up.[17] The researchers suggest that children who grow up in poverty are especially likely to be around smokers, to find smoking regarded as normal behavior, and have the ready availability of cigarettes to experiment with. Since most people in their social world smoke, including their parents and friends, smokers rationalize why shouldn't they smoke as well if they enjoy it? Smoking also serves the purposes of managing stress and coping with the strain of material deprivation. Additionally, poor people are likely to be less informed about the dangers of smoking, which means if they do smoke, they are likely to continue. Furthermore, Jarvis and Wardle find that the poor achieve higher levels of nicotine intake because they smoke more cigarettes and smoke them more intensely. All these circumstances are linked to being poor and reinforce smoking among the socioeconomically deprived populations.

Jarvis and Wardle thus conclude that stressful conditions, material deprivation, and adverse socioeconomic conditions induce the poor to smoke. "This illustrates what might be proposed as a general law of Western society, namely, that any marker of disadvantage, whether personal, material or cultural, is likely to have an independent association with cigarette smoking."[18] Growing up in a household where one or both parents smoke, having a smoking spouse, or regularly socializing with smokers also invites smoking in a social context. These situations are more common among the poor. Of course, some affluent people likewise smoke and their reasons may be different than those previously identified—although stress is a likely culprit for everybody. Smoking among the affluent does not change the fact that this risk behavior is unusual at the higher levels of society and that the smoking habit is concentrated among lower-strata groups, especially the lower class.

Conclusion

There is a social pattern to smoking, which indicates that smoking is not a random, individual decision completely independent of structural influences. As Jarvis and Wardle observe, smoking, along with drinking alcohol and drug use, is an individual risk behavior that involves an element of personal choice. However, smoking and other risky behaviors have not been viewed in a broad social context by researchers as much as they have been characterized as situations of individual personal responsibility. If people wish to avoid the negative effects of smoking on their health, it is therefore reasoned that they should not smoke. If they choose to smoke, what happens to them is no one's fault but their own. This victim-blaming approach, argue Jarvis and Wardle, is not helpful, because it does not explain why disadvantaged people are drawn to poor health habits like smoking and the types of social conditions that promote this behavior.[19]

Stages of a Smoker's Career

Sociologist Jason Hughes suggests that smokers pass through five stages in their smoking career: (1) becoming a smoker, (2) continued smoking, (3) regular smoking, (4) addicted smoking, and, for some, (5) stopping smoking.[20] Based on interviews with both smokers and ex-smokers in Great Britain, Hughes finds that the first experience people have with smoking cigarettes in the initial stage of *becoming a smoker* is typically unpleasant. The smoker usually feels nauseated. One respondent told Hughes that she really did not like her first cigarette, describing it as "foul."[21] This raises a basic question: If the first experience is so nasty, why do people continue? Hughes answer is that people learn how to smoke by having other individuals interpret the experience for them and tell them how to distinguish the desired effects from the undesirable. Specifically, they learn how to inhale properly and pull the smoke down into their lungs, as well as how much to smoke and how frequently they should do it. One woman in the Hughes study reported on what it was like being a smoker when she first started:

> I don't know, it was quite exciting, I thought I'd grown up! It was something new. And it is a skill that you have to learn to do it properly so that people don't say, "she's not inhaling properly, she's not smoking." You have to learn how to do it.[22]

Hughes points out that, in the beginning, smoking is a social activity carried on with other people. It typically has its origins in adolescent peer groups, in which teens imitate adult behavior. Teens smoke to "connect with," "fit in," and "impress" their friends. Joy Johnson and her associates also observed the social nature of teen smoking.[23] This study, conducted in Canada, determined that adolescents are more socially than physically dependent on cigarettes in the beginning. The social setting, namely relaxing with peers, promoted smoking more than the cigarettes. Often the teens did not smoke when their friends were not around. But when friends were present, new smokers used cigarettes primarily to connect with them socially, project an image of being "cool," and show solidarity. Three teenagers in the study analyzed smoking in their peer group in the following way:

> Like it [smoking] is a social aspect of their life that they have become dependent on, as much as the nicotine, you know. I think almost the social setting of it [smoking] is something that is somewhat addictive itself [17-year-old female].[24] People don't really have to smoke, but they do it anyways to like fit in, or whatever, and they smoke to put out an image to people [17-year-old male].[25] It's more what you will do to fit in, not what you will do to smoke, because you may not actually want to smoke [16-year-old male].[26]

Hughes provides another example of the influence of sociability on the first stage of smoking as reflected in the comments of an older man recalling his initial use of cigarettes:

> It was part of talking, very much part of talking with other people and the intimacies with other people, you know, sitting in a car, waiting for something to happen, share a cigarette, in a group of people talking, articulating. And it was certainly something to do with getting on with members of the opposite sex, that was also something you did by offering cigarettes and you shared a cigarette, it was part of the process of interaction. I liked it, the taste was okay. . . . But it was the "social process" that always brought it back to me, kept me a smoker during that stage [51-year-old male].[27]

Reports such as these and others support Hughes's contention that the beginning stage of becoming a smoker is principally a social experience. Not only are the techniques of smoking learned within peer groups, but the act of smoking is used to promote social relationships, reinforce personal bonds, and express group affiliation. Some teens in the study by Johnson and her colleagues also smoked because they felt empowered by smoking in social situations.[28] Teenagers who had cigarettes, for example, felt power over those without them. Those with cigarettes picked whom they would or would not share cigarettes with, and enjoyed being selective. Others simply felt powerful by the act of smoking. One adolescent described:

> It's you doing it, like your own cigarette. You're smoking it. It's nobody else saying you have to do it or you can't do this, it's your choice. It gives you a little more power, kind of [15-year-old male].[29]

Johnson and her colleagues found that another reason that adolescents smoke is the effect of the nicotine on their emotions. Smoking helped them feel "calm" and reduced anxiety. It could also ease depression, sadness, fear, loneliness, and anger. Several respondents in this study indicated that they smoked when they were upset about something. Smoking soothed or suppressed emotional discomfort. The study also found that some teens smoke simply because they like it, and to them smoking was a "treat"—much like having a chocolate bar every now and then. Others regarded smoking as a sign of the transition to an adult social identity, as the teenager sets out to establish a sense of self independent of his or her parents. Hughes observed that some parents strongly opposed smoking. One teen's father got up and left a restaurant if someone were smoking. But the teen smoked anyway to signal an independent course and rebellion against parental authority.

While numerous reasons influence an adolescent to try a cigarette and many—perhaps most—do at some point in growing up, the majority do not continue. For those that do, however, they enter the second stage described by Hughes, that of *continued smoking*. In this stage, beginning smokers not only start smoking more frequently, the increased smoking becomes part of a consistent pattern of behavior. These smokers continue to use cigarettes to socialize, but now for other reasons too, including gaining pleasure, alleviating stress, or helping their concentration at work. In this stage, they now also smoke when they are alone, instead of just when they are with other people. As one respondent tells Hughes about why he continued to smoke when he was younger:

> I started to use cigarettes to deal with stress much more, in a sense it was dealing with stress before, but it was dealing with oiling the wheels in the social situation. Something to do in the social context. But I started to smoke much more on my own, when I was working, when I was under pressure of some kind or another, if I had something to do, a big deadline, I'd buy some cigarettes and sit and smoke and work on it [51-year-old male].[30]

The dominant themes that Hughes finds in the second stage of continued smoking are that the smokers (1) increasingly smoke when alone, (2) begin recognizing themselves as smokers, (3) smoke to control their emotional feelings, and (4) realize they feel a longing or need for tobacco during the day. A major part of the smoking experience at this time is a growing feeling of dependence on nicotine.

The third stage is that of *regular smoker*. Now smoking is clearly a lifestyle habit. It is the time when Hughes says tobacco use has become a central part of the smoker's identity. The user is also typically familiar with different types of cigarettes, those with or without filters, menthol, and so forth. The user chooses a particular brand for a variety of reasons, such as cost, availability, image, type of filter, taste, length, amount of tar and nicotine, and so on. The respondents in Hughes' study clearly understood that the brand they smoked was a marker of their identity. Some picked brands to smoke that seemed to have the least health risk in relation to the amount of tar and nicotine they contained. Others picked brands that allowed them to identify themselves as tough or sophisticated. Still others preferred how some cigarettes taste. One respondent commented:

> They [menthol cigarettes] taste nice, it's like when you have a menthol cigarette it feels like you're breathing fresh air instead of tobacco. And they don't leave a bad taste in your mouth afterwards, not that I can tell [23-year-old female].[31]

The smokers also understood the health risks, but smoked anyway. In Hughes's view, they embraced the risk of smoking as an act of defiance. Being told they shouldn't smoke and not being allowed to smoke in certain places, they found a place to smoke as an act of defiance or expression of their individual freedom. For example, on an airplane a steward told one female respondent that she could not smoke where she was seated. The steward offered to move her to a seat in the rear where she could smoke, but the area was crowded and she would have been wedged in-between two other people. She rationalized that she had paid her fare like everybody else and had a right to enjoy the flight. "But I was determined that I was going to smoke simply because I was not allowed to," stated the woman.[32] She resented the way the steward had informed her she could not smoke, his manner implying that people who smoked should be treated as "lepers." So she waited an hour and a half and lit up another cigarette when the steward was not looking. Another woman described her own attitude about smoking:

> But if I want a cigarette, I will smoke. The more people tell me I shouldn't smoke, the more I smoke. Quite literally, I have this thing that "I am me" and if I want to smoke, I will smoke. I don't obviously smoke in people's houses—friends' houses—if they don't like smoking. You have to respect their views, obviously. My doctor says I shouldn't smoke because I have had two heart attacks and I have angina. I've had two heart operations but I still smoke [53-year-old female].[33]

Other regular smokers indicated they smoked to stabilize their moods. For example, they used cigarettes to help them feel less lethargic in the morning when they woke up, or to relax when they felt stressed or overworked. A particular theme of regular smokers, according to Hughes, was the increasing use of tobacco as a means of self-control. Cigarettes had become a method to reduce stress and anxiety. But regardless of the reasons for smoking regularly, Hughes maintains that, in time, the desire to smoke becomes a more compelling influence than the individual will power of the smoker.

This emotional state signals the entry of the smoker into the fourth stage of *addicted smoking*. What makes this stage unique, in Hughes' view, is that the need for a cigarette is experienced as a preoccupation—literally an obsession—to smoke. Hughes describes cases in which respondents were obsessed with having a cigarette. They had to smoke before they did anything else. This was especially so if they had to do something as well as they could. The cigarette became a friend because it provided security; it was an emotional resource for coping with day-to-day events. Thus, the addicted smoker used cigarettes to handle stress, make the transition from one activity to another, be a reward for something well done, and a source of comfort when feeling anxious. "From the psychological point of view it is mind over matter," states a 35-year-old woman in the Hughes study, "your head is completely dominating you now, that you must have a cigarette."[34]

Johnson and her associates describe the stage of being addicted as one in which smokers cannot think clearly without cigarettes and plan their day around opportunities to smoke. One adolescent in this study stated she first became aware she was addicted to nicotine when, at the age of 13, she felt compelled to walk two hours to a store to buy cigarettes. When a cigarette is smoked, particularly after a period of abstinence, the smoker at this stage experiences a strong sense of relief. Addicted smokers often smoke to feel "normal." Here is how some described their full-fledged dependence on tobacco:

> Addiction is something that takes over a whole person's self-being. . . . Like I said, I have friends that can't have a conversation or even go on with their everyday life until they know that they are going to have a cigarette soon [16-year-old female].[35]
>
> It's gone beyond maybe wanting it or enjoying it, but at this point, your body is addicted to it, and no matter what, you couldn't get through the day without either thinking about it or feeling like you need a cigarette [19-year-old female].[36]

Hughes explains that the final stage, the fifth, is that of *stopping smoking*. The smell and taste of cigarettes, social criticism and rejection, and the danger to health are all reasons for giving up smoking. Of course, not every smoker reaches this stage. But many do, and for those who successfully make the transition from smoker to former smoker, the process is often difficult. Times of the day when the person usually smoked (e.g., on awakening, at meals) are stressful reminders to have a cigarette. Spending time with friends who smoke is likewise difficult. As a 28-year-old male in the Hughes study recalled: "If I sat down for a drink in a pub with a friend who smoked, it drove me insane."[37] Some smokers stop smoking, but the attempt (or attempts) end in failure. The reminders and stress of not smoking are too much for them to handle, so they return to their cigarettes. Those who stop smoking and resist all further temptations, according to Hughes, are people who are able to stop thinking about smoking and no longer associate smoking with stressful events.

Social situations are also important in smoking cessation. Laurier and his colleagues, for example, found that some people stop smoking when the social activity promoting cigarette use ceased.[38] Changing employment or membership in a social group could bring an end to smoking, for example, when the individual moved out of a group of smokers into a group of nonsmokers. Laurier and his colleagues therefore suggest that once the social context of smoking is no longer meaningful, the act of smoking can be more readily abandoned, as shown by the following account of a 30-year-old married woman who stopped smoking:

> Well, I got bored with it. I didn't enjoy it. Ehm, my husband at that point was quite asthmatic and I thought I was going to kill him. So that was another reason. I'd just had enough really. It was just something that I was doing when I was out doing wild things and partying. I was stopping that as well and so I stopped smoking. I had a really bad cold one day, and I thought right I won't smoke today. And then I thought I'm not going to smoke tomorrow either. And I just carried on.[39]

Other people stop smoking because they no longer wish to put their health at risk or risk the health of others around them who might inhale their smoke as well. For a woman, becoming pregnant and being a parent (for a man too) can curtail smoking. So people are able to stop, even when addicted, and the social context in which they live their lives is a factor in the decision to stop, as it is in the decision to begin smoking.

Conclusion: Smoking As Risk Taking

Smoking was almost an exclusively male practice in the United States until the 1940s, when women began smoking in large numbers. The catalyst for this change was women's entry into the labor market in World War II to replace men who had left for the military. However, recognition of the health risks associated with smoking has driven down the percentages of smokers among both sexes, but more so among men. The reduction in smoking among women is impeded by younger women taking up cigarettes as older women quit. Today fewer than 25 percent of all men and about 21 percent of women are smokers. Black men are more likely to smoke than white men, but white women are more likely to smoke than black women. Age remains an important variable because smoking usually begins in adolescence and is associated with the influence of peers. Another especially powerful variable is social class in that people in the upper- and upper-middle classes typically do not smoke. Smoking is more common in the lower-middle and working class, and especially prevalent in the lower class because its practice is increasingly defined by the larger society as socially unacceptable.

We have seen that people smoke for a variety of reasons. They usually try cigarettes or some other form of nicotine as a teenager and do so as a social activity with peers. They smoke to fit in and be part of their peer group. Those who continue to smoke do so because they enjoy the physiological effects, and/or find it helps them to relax and cope with stress. But are these reasons for smoking enough to counteract the well-known fact that smoking is bad for your health? Obviously, for some people they are.

Hughes helps us to understand this situation by concluding that smoking is a means by which some individuals like to think they are defying death. Since the diseases caused by smoking develop over time and occur mainly in older people, for the young smoker a death due to smoking is something that lies far into the future. And the damage that smoking does to the body is not only long-term, it is also invisible to other people in day-to-day social interaction. These smokers rationalize they can risk their health in return for current pleasures, since the risk of death can be temporarily put aside. Thus, some people smoke because it is a risk-taking activity. Hughes states:

> Crucially, it [smoking] is a risk for later in life, and not for the here and now. It can be seen as a way of *expressing* that "I am not investing in my future, I'm *living for now*."[40]

Hughes observes that if death from smoking-related causes were more immediate and the effects of tobacco on the body more noticeable from the beginning, the history of smoking might be far different. Obviously, fewer people would smoke.

Returning to the model of risk-taking behavior (see Figure 1-1 in Chapter 1) discussed in the first chapter, the responses of regular smokers to the risks posed by tobacco use would generally be that of *passive acceptance*. Persons in the passive acceptance mode have a somewhat greater capacity for agency (choice) and are not as constrained by structure as those in *passive denial,* with little or no choice about how they can cope with risk. Those in passive acceptance could take action to abort the risk, but do not. They know smoking harms their health and that their life can be curtailed because of it, yet they passively accept the risk and continue to smoke. Why? Because they enjoy it for both physiological and social reasons that are reinforced by their addiction. The "spike" in the brain after inhalation and the manner in which cigarettes help create a relaxed mood and facilitate social interaction with other smokers is a desired state of being. As one teenage Hispanic female explains:

> It [smoking cigarettes] . . . gives you a buzz. It . . . feels good. It like drowns all your worries. It'd like you know they're still going to be there, but they're just like, they're gone for the moment. I don't know how to explain it. [It does] . . . something to me, it's just like a release—it's just like it releases all my problems. I don't think about them when I'm doing it, nothing. It's like, I don't know. It's weird because like . . . the cigarette is your friend. It's like you don't have a friend in the world or something, and then you just go and you light up the cigarette and it's like everybody's your friend.[41]

Ceasing to smoke, in contrast, is unpleasant because the body experiences symptoms of withdrawal and cravings that diminish the motivation to quit. The unseen damage to lungs and the cardiovascular system can be ignored for years until the harm eventually becomes self-evident. What is not apparent can be ignored until some future time when the bill comes due in the form of lung cancer, heart disease, or some other smoking-related affliction.

Notes

1. Martin J. Jarvis and Wardle. 1999. "Social Patterning of Individual Health Behaviours: The Case of Cigarette Smoking." In Michael Marmot and Richard G. Wilkinson (eds.), *Social Determinants of Health.* Oxford, UK: Oxford University Press, pp. 240–255; R. Rogers and E. Powell-Griner. 1991. "Life Expectancies of Cigarette Smokers and Nonsmokers in the United States," *Social Science and Medicine,* 32: 1151–1159; Catherine E. Ross and Chia-ling Wu. 1995. "The Links Between Education and Health," *American Sociological Review,* 42: 258–276.
2. Centers for Disease Control and Prevention. 2002. "Annual Smoking-Attributable Mortality, Years of Potential Life Lost, and Economic

Costs—United States, 1995–1999." *Morbidity and Mortality Report*, 51: 300–302.

3. Avram Goldstein. 2001. *Addiction: From Biology to Drug Policy*. Oxford, UK: University of Oxford Press.

4. Eric Laurier, Linda McKee, and Norma Goodwin. 2000. "Daily and Life-course Contexts of Smoking." *Sociology of Health & Illness*, 22: 289–309.

5. Goldstein, p. 122.

6. Ibid.

7. Ibid., p. 125.

8. Ibid., pp. 127–128.

9. Ibid.

10. Jarvis and Wardle, p. 244.

11. Rob McGee and Warren R. Stanton. 1993. "A Longitudinal Study of Reasons for Smoking in Adolescence." *Addictions*, 88: 265–271.

12. Diana Chapman Walsh, Glorian Sorensen, and Lori Leonard. 1995. "Gender, Health, and Cigarette Smoking." In B. Amick, S. Levine, A. Tarlov, and D. Walsh (eds.), *Society and Health*. New York: Oxford University Press, p. 151.

13. Ibid., p. 153.

14. Ibid., pp. 131–171.

15. Center for Health Statistics. 2002. *Health, United States, 2002*. Washington, D.C.: U.S. Government Printing Office.

16. Andrew Adonis and Stephen Pollard. 1997. *A Class Act: The Myth of Britain's Classless Society*. London: Penguin.

17. Jarvis and Wardle, p. 246.

18. Ibid., p. 242.

19. Ibid., p. 241.

20. Jason Hughes. 2003. *Learning to Smoke: Tobacco Use in the West*. Chicago: University of Chicago Press.

21. Ibid., p. 148.

22. Ibid., p. 149.

23. Joy L. Johnson, Joan L. Bottorff, Barbara Moffat, Pamela A. Ratner, Jean A. Shoveller, and Chris Y. Lovato. 2003. "Tobacco Dependence: Adolescents: Perspectives on the Need to Smoke." *Social Science & Medicine*, 56: 1481–1492.

24. Ibid., p. 1484.

25. Ibid., p. 1485.

26. Ibid.

27. Hughes, pp. 153–154.

28. Johnson et al., pp. 1486–1487.

29. Ibid., p. 1487.

30. Hughes, p. 154.

31. Ibid., pp. 161–162.
32. Ibid., p. 163.
33. Ibid., p. 162.
34. Ibid., p. 170.
35. Johnson et al., p. 1488.
36. Ibid.
37. Hughes, p. 173.
38. Laurier et al.
39. Ibid., p. 302.
40. Hughes, p. 135.
41. Gilbert Quintero and Sally Davis. 2002. "Why Do Teens Smoke? American Indian and Hispanic Adolescents' Perspectives on Functional Values and Addiction." *Medical Anthropology Quarterly,* 16: 439–457.

Extreme Sports

The lifestyle risks previously discussed in this book involved decisions about practices that reduce the lifespan through disease. Heart disease, cancer, AIDS, and a host of other health problems can be the result, if the decision is "yes." Extreme sports are different. They are the leisure pursuit of thrills. Extreme sports, also known as alternative sports or action sports, are highly intense, individualistic sporting activities carried out by physically fit people who deliberately risk their lives and limbs to accomplish some often spectacular and thrilling sporting technique. These sports include extreme skiing, in which skiers descend from one snow-covered ledge to another down a mountain, cliff parachuting, and Moto-X (motorcycle jumping off ski ramps). There is also downhill mountain biking (at speeds as high as 60 miles per hour), bungee jumping, base jumping (parachuting off buildings, antenna towers, and bridge spans), ice climbing (up frozen waterfalls and cliffs), pond swooping (parachuting into ponds and skimming across the top at 70 miles per hour), and risky versions of mountain climbing, rock climbing, snowboarding, river rafting, surfing, and similar activities. Extreme sports are a way to live life on the edge where one mistake can be fatal or result in serious injury. "Undertaken at great height or at great speed," observes anthropologist Catherine Palmer, "these high-risk sports are not for the faint-hearted."[1]

Sports Illustrated, for example, had this to say about an up and coming 18-year-old free-skier:

> In a sport in which grizzled veterans often aren't old enough to drive, [he] . . . is a bit long in the tooth to be touted as the next big thing. His age, though, has yet to affect his good judgment—he still doesn't have any. The self-described "addict for adrenaline" specializes in the slopestyle (skiing over obstacles such as rails and tables) and big air (the name says it all) disciplines. In his signature big air jump, the Rodeo, he completes two helicopter spins with his body parallel to the ground.[2]

Some extreme sports, like certain snowboarding events and mogul skiing, are now Olympic sports. On just one day of the 2003 Winter Olympics at Salt Lake City, extreme sports athletes won seven medals for the United States, with a sweep of the top three finishers in the men's and a gold in the women's halfpipe snowboarding, two silvers in the men's and women's moguls, and a bronze in the men's slalom snowboarding. After the men's halfpipe sweep, a spectator with a video camera jokingly approached the silver medallist and asked if he was going to go home and smoke crack? The snowboarder:

> . . . smiled at his goofball buddy and gleefully played along. "Dude," he answered, "I'm gonna smoke the fattest. . . ." Then [he] noticed the man with a NEWSWEEK media credential standing next to him and scribbling on his notepad. "Dude, nice try!" He said to his pal. "You almost got me, man! Drugs are bad! I've gotta go take a drug test! I love drug tests."[3]

Another extreme sport is base jumping, or parachuting from a structure on the ground. The people who do it are sometimes killed, such as the legendary 32-year-old Norwegian known as the "Human Fly" for his string of successful parachute jumps off high structures. Jumping off a tall cliff in Norway in a fog in June 1999, he died when winds flung him back against the cliff. The following is a brief description of this sport:

> Their extreme sport is called BASE-jumping, whose acronymic name derives from the four types of structures that its unusual athletes leap from—buildings, antennas, spans (bridges), and earth (cliffs). Equipped with rectangular canopy chutes, toggles for steering, a knowledge of which way the wind is blowing, no reserve chutes (as compared with skydivers), and a special arrangement of brain cells, participants jump to conclusions from great and forbidden heights, or from little ones where a chute has little time to open. Until they release their chutes, they fall at 60 m.p.h. The end is often unsatisfactory.[4]

Why do people take such risks? These sports can be extremely dangerous, yet they are willingly undertaken. Why this is so is not fully known, but the available answers will be presented in this chapter. Unfortunately, this topic has received little attention from social scientists, which means the research literature currently available on it is limited. Whereas subjects like alcohol and drug abuse are characterized by extensive theoretical applications, these are not found in extreme sports.

Moreover, it is not known how many people actually participate in extreme sports. Existing estimates do, however, suggest these sports are popular among youth and young adults and that the number of participants is believed to be rising. For instance, during the 1990s, snowboarding participation is estimated to have increased from 1.8 to 3.6 million people, rock climbing from 4.9 to 9.3 million, while the number of mountain bike owners doubled from 4 million to 8 million.[5]

Marketing reports as well indicate that extreme sports are very popular among the so-called Generation Y, persons born between 1977 and 1994.[6] Interest is high enough to attract sponsors and media coverage for extreme sports, since Generation Y represents a sizable market—some 23 percent of the American population. Every year, ESPN broadcasts on national television the X Games, in which athletes compete for over $1 million in prize money. According to one report:

> Andrew . . . isn't your typical couch potato. The 26-year-old from Cleveland, who works two jobs to finance his new mortgage payments, rarely sits glued to the tube—even when his hometown Cleveland Browns, is playing on Monday Night Football. But when the X Games or the Gravity Games are on, [he] not only makes time to watch, he actually schedules his day around what's on TV. "These athletes are so on the edge that it actually makes watching TV enjoyable," [says he], who hung up his skis more than 10 years ago in favor of a snowboard. "Extreme sports are my Monday Night Football."[7]

Another man who attended the X Games as a doubtful spectator described his conversion to ardent fan:

> Before rummaging through my backpack at the security checkpoint . . . , the first morning of the Winter X Games, a cop posed this question: "Alcoholic beverages?" I told him thanks but no thanks, I'd wait till lunchtime. The truth was, you don't need beers to catch a buzz at these, the seventh Winter X Games, held at Aspen's Buttermilk Mountain. All you had to do was head over to the SnoCross venue and breathe deeply.
>
> SnoCross . . . is a race of modified snowmobiles over a course featuring numerous bumps and jumps. I'll admit, on that first morning my initial attitude toward this "sport" was in need of substantial clarification. What, I wondered could be enjoyable about watching a bunch of cacophonous contraptions put enough exhaust in the air to stupefy a fair-sized reggae festival?
>
> That was before I saw any of the guys come hurtling off the monster jump at the end of the first lap—the one that threw them 125 feet out and three stories high. . . . It was loud, it was noxious, it could not have been more anomalous at this once-tranquil resort, renowned for its elevated environmental consciousness. It was also pretty freakin' cool.[8]

Obviously extreme sports can be thrilling. The best explanation suggests thrill-seeking or an "adrenaline rush" is the basic motivation for participation. But, as stated, the extent to which this is true and whether other factors are involved await clarification. Marketing research shows that the average American "thrill-seeker" is male, between the ages of 18 to 34 years, living in the West, unmarried, has less than three years of college, and an income of either between $40,000 and $60,000, or over $100,000 annually.[9] The manner in which risk has been commercialized in extreme sports will be discussed in the next section, followed by additional demographic data about extreme sports participants and a discussion of the relevant theories explaining why people are willing to take the risks.

The Commercialization of Risk

Extreme sports in the United States represents, as indicated, a large market. Besides television coverage and organized competition for prize money, the world of extreme sports also includes magazines like *On the Edge* (climbing), *Thrasher* and *Slam* (skateboarding), *Carve* and *Rip Tide* (surfing), and *Powder Hound* and *Ballistic* (skiing) and videos like "Coming at Ya Hyper" (rock climbing). Extreme sports also boast an extensive array of special clothing and sports equipment, such as gloves, sunglasses, T-shirts, helmets, protective padding, mountain bikes, snowboards, parachutes, karabiners, surf wax, and so on.[10] The expense associated with extreme sports can be considerable, especially when the costs of equipment and travel are added in.

Another marketing sector promoting extreme sports is adventure travel. The travel industry estimates that about 620,000 persons take what is known as "hard-adventure vacations" each year.[11] Typically, the clientele for these specialized vacations is male, relatively young (average age is mid-30s), unmarried, well educated (most have attended college), and with high household incomes ($50,000 or more). Palmer describes the extreme sports population as a whole: "Ranging from weekend warriors who do no training, have little skills and are content to infrequently subject themselves to the waves, the single tracks and the *col* faces of the great outdoors, through to hard-core practitioners who are fully assimilated into the argot, fashion and technical skill of their preferred discipline, the extreme sports market is indeed a hotchpotch of interests and expertise."[12]

The clientele for adventure companies are typically the weekend warriors or first-time participants, both with little or no experience with these pursuits. Adventure companies package dangerous activities like mountain climbing, river rafting, skydiving, and the like into a relatively safe experience by providing ample safety measures, controlling the environment as much as possible, and ensuring that skilled professional guides are available to prevent emergencies or, if they arise, act swiftly. Palmer explains that the contemporary adventure experience is one in which the

adventure traveler can live on the "edge" without meeting any misfortune. Yet misfortune can and does occur. Skydivers, base jumpers, mountain climbers, white-water rafters, and others are sometimes killed or injured. Palmer describes two such disasters: Interlaken in 1999 and Mount Everest in 1996.

Interlaken 1999

Interlaken is a small village in Switzerland near the Saxtenbach Gorge, famed for its white-water rafting through a steep, narrow canyon. "The sheer cliffs of the gorge meant that scrambling to safety should the river suddenly surge was not an option," notes Palmer.[13] One day in August, 1999, 45 clients who paid $75 for the 90-minute "canyonning adventure of a lifetime" and eight guides descended into the Gorge. But a sudden change in the weather and a heavy downpour caused the gorge to rapidly fill with water. Deep in the gorge, the participants had only a constricted view of the weather above them and the water upstream that was crashing toward them. Eighteen tourists and three guides were swept to their death by the flash flood that engulfed them.

Mount Everest 1996

The 1996 Mount Everest disaster happened in May of that year when a storm created conditions leading to the deaths of eight people. This event involved both clients and their professional guides, which Palmer finds to be an important variable in the outcome. The clients were weekend climbers who paid $65,000 each for the experience of climbing the world's tallest mountain. "Despite their physical limitations," concludes Palmer, "lack of climbing experience, and the very real dangers posed by the inclement weather, the fact that these weekend mountaineers had paid extraordinary sums of money seemingly bought them the right to risk not only their own lives, but those of their Western and Sherpa guides too." She points out that—on Everest—safety hinges on speed. Climbers need to reach the top and descend to their last camp before they run out of oxygen or are overtaken by darkness. But on the day of the disaster, according to Palmer, some weekend climbers hampered by fatigue and altitude sickness caused their climbing parties to advance too slowly to the summit. Yet everyone pressed on.

Palmer suggests the reason for pushing to the top was to give the novices their money's worth. For instance, one of the weekend climbers was a middle-age male postal worker whose boyhood dream was to climb Mount Everest. He had worked at two jobs to save the money to pay for the trip. Since he and the other clients had paid a great amount of money to reach the summit, it is speculated that the guides were intent on getting them there if possible. Jon Krakauer, who wrote a book about the Everest disaster, *Into Thin Air*, was one of the clients.[14] He says he does not know why the leaders of the climbing parties did not turn back. Perhaps they did not recognize the weather was deteriorating. Krakauer recalled that, in his oxygen-depleted mind, the clouds he saw drifting toward the summit "looked innocuous, wispy, insubstantial."[15] Krakauer was obviously fortunate. He survived, but some of his colleagues, including the postal worker, did not. Krakauer was one of the first climbers in his group to reach the top, and this made an important difference as events began to unfold. He writes:

> Straddling the top of the world, one foot in China and the other in Nepal, I cleared the ice from my oxygen mask, hunched a shoulder against the wind, and stared absently down at the vastness of Tibet. I understood on some dim, detached level that the sweep of earth beneath my feet was a spectacular sight. I'd been fantasizing about this moment, and the release of emotion that would accompany it, for many months. But now that I was finally here, actually standing on the summit of Mount Everest, I just couldn't summon the energy to care.[16]

Krakauer had not slept in 57 hours and over the past few days had been able to eat only a bowl of noodle soup and some peanut M&Ms. Moreover, he had two separated ribs that made breathing in what little oxygen he had left in his tank difficult. He felt cold, tired, and apprehensive about the long, dangerous descent. Krakauer took some photos and then headed down after spending less than five minutes at the top of the world. He writes:

> A moment later, I paused to take another photo, this one looking down the Southeast Ridge, the route we had ascended. Training my lens on a pair of climbers approaching the summit, I noticed something that until that moment had escaped my attention. To the south, where the sky had been perfectly clear just an hour earlier, a blanket of clouds now hid Pumori, Ama Dablam, and the lesser peaks surrounding Everest.[17]

As Krakauer began his descent, he was extremely anxious because he was running low on oxygen. His situation worsened when he had to step over to one side to let about dozen climbers go past him on their ascent toward the peak. They moved past him at a snail's pace because of the high altitude. In the meantime, Krakauer was getting frantic. He asked another climber to turn his oxygen regulator off to conserve air, but the climber had mistakenly turned the valve open to full flow and soon Krakauer was out of oxygen. He ripped his oxygen mask off because he was suffocating and struggled down to the South Summit where fresh oxygen cylinders had been placed. He noticed the weather was no longer so benign and visibility was disappearing as he left the South Summit to continue his descent to the camp.

> Four hundred vertical feet above, where the summit was still washed in bright sunlight under an immaculate cobalt sky, my compadres dallied to memorialize their arrival at the apex of the planet, unfurling flags and snapping photos, using up precious ticks of the clock. None of them imagined that a horrible ordeal was drawing nigh. Nobody suspected that by the end of that long day, every minute would matter.[18]

Krakauer descended into clouds and light snow. He had difficulty seeing ahead of him and weather conditions only worsened as he continued down. The storm turned into a full-scale blizzard with winds gusting as high as 60 knots, but Krakauer had already covered the most treacherous terrain immediately in front of him. Nevertheless, the rest of his trek downward to the first camp below the summit was not easy, especially near the end when he had to maneuver down an ice-covered incline while exhausted. Finally, he reached the camp, found his tent, and lunged into it, more tired than he had ever been in his entire life. He had done it! He had climbed Mount Everest and now he was safe. All in all, it had been a great day despite the hardships, he thought, as he tried to keep warm and drifted in and out of consciousness, delirious from exhaustion, dehydration, and sustained oxygen depletion.

Not until several hours later, when he was awakened to join a search party, did Krakauer learn that some in his party had been stranded by the storm. Eight people died, but only six bodies were ever located. What happened to the two missing climbers has never been determined. They simply disappeared. The survivors made it back to the camp. Some walked in on their own; others were helped down by their colleagues. Many had frostbitten limbs. One of the climbing party leaders managed to call his pregnant wife and talk to her before dying from exposure. He had remained high on the mountain to help a client—the postal worker—who was too incapacitated by fatigue and sickness to descend, and then found that he was too exhausted to move as well when it became dark and the temperature dropped. Another fatality was a 47-year-old Japanese woman, who was the oldest woman to ever reach the summit. Krakauer says that it became clear to him later that few of the clients on the peak that day (including himself), realized the seriousness of the risks they faced and the thinness of the margin by which life is sustained above 25,000 feet. He concludes:

> . . . it is easy to lose sight of the fact that climbing mountains will never be a safe, predictable, rule-bound enterprise. This is an activity that idealizes risk-taking; the sports most celebrated figures have always been those who stick their necks out the farthest and manage to get away with it. Climbers, as a species, are simply not distinguished by an excess of prudence. And that holds especially true for Everest climbers: when presented with a chance to reach the planet's highest summit, history shows, people are surprisingly quick to abandon good judgment.[19]

The total number of people who died on Mount Everest during 1996 was 12, with Krakauer's expedition having the largest number of deaths of any climbing party that year. Yet despite the fatalities, adventure travel companies continue to accept paying clients today and lead them up Mount Everest. The attraction of being able to scale the world's highest mountain and the feeling of accomplishment associated with it continues to overcome fear of the risks involved.

Age and Gender

People who engage in extreme sports appear to be a special breed, a collection of individuals who thrive on risk taking. While there is little data on the social and demographic characteristics of this group, the great majority of extreme sports participants apparently range in age from adolescence to the mid-30s. Athletic skills typically decline between the ages of 25 and 35 years, and this is true for extreme sports participants as well. Beginning in a person's mid-20s, the heart can no longer pump blood as fast as before, neither can the lungs put oxygen into the blood as quickly. In addition, the body's tissues are unable to extract oxygen from the blood as efficiently and cells are not as capable of using oxygen after they receive it. Bones and joints also start deteriorating at this time. Extreme sports are therefore a young person's game, with physical capabilities peaking between the ages of 16 and 24 years.

Statistics on the ratio of male to females in extreme sports are also lacking, but the general observation is that such activities are predominantly male. As John Derbyshire puts it: "Female gamblers, female speculators, female practitioners of extreme sports, female explorers, female soldiers are a scattered few."[20] Derbyshire adds that females tend to prefer security and have a lower appetite for risk than males. Consequently, males vastly outnumber females in extreme sports. Not surprisingly, then, the subculture that now surrounds extreme sports is also male-oriented. A study of snowboarding found, for example, that male participants have deliberately invented a masculine environment for their sport's culture.[21] This showed in four specific social practices: (1) linking snowboarding to masculine cultural images in other sports, (2) masculine styles of social interaction and clothing, (3) expressions of aggression, and (4) an emphasis on heterosexuality.

Yet some females do participate in snowboarding and other extreme sports, and there is research suggesting that, over time, the masculine emphasis in the extreme sports subculture will change as the number of women participants continues to increase.[22] Joanne Kay maintains that, given the attraction of adolescent girls to extreme sports despite its masculine bias and the recent history of women's incursion into traditional sports and their appropriation of male sport culture, extreme sports will likely become less masculine in its cultural orientation.[23] The notion of risk as a condition of participation in extreme sports, Kay believes, is more a product of a generalized youth sport culture instead of an exclusively male sport culture. That some women can be as interested in risky sports as are some men, is seen in this account of a woman skier:

> [She] is a hard-core addict, and she knows it. Ever since her first childhood schuss down a snow-covered peak, she has been hopelessly hooked on adrenalin. In her teens, she abandoned the cozy confines of ski resorts for the 70-degree inclines and 50-foot drops of rugged wilderness trails. By her early 20s, she was the nation's foremost female "radical skier," the darling of cinematographers eager to capture her perilous cliff jumps and set them to rock soundtracks for the MTV crowd.

> Today, six knee operations later, [she] is paid by sponsors to ski down the world's tallest, remotest mountains, from Tajikistan to New Zealand. To relax, she scales towering rock formations. She has snuck into Tibet for some serious mountaineering and biked solo across India. Perversely, she says she gets a thrill from virtually any kind of risk: Hitchhiking through the desolate Alaskan interior, she was picked up by a man who threatened her life. "I got a kick out of it," she says.[24]

Extreme sports are primarily activities for the affluent, especially the middle class. These sports require sufficient leisure time to practice and perform them. Competitive contests take additional time. Equipment, as well as travel to suitable locations, as noted, can be expensive too. For these reasons,, extreme sports are not typically performed by people from the lower class. Indeed, existing accounts confirm that extreme sports are largely a middle class activity, although there are exceptions, such as motorcycle racing, which largely attracts working-class participants.[25]

Thrill-Seeking Personalities

Risk-takers in extreme sports have been characterized by psychologists as people who turn to this type of activity because they are bored with conventional lives and jobs. They seek the thrills that come with taking risks in dangerous activities. Often they take multiple risks, not just in sports but in other areas of their lives as well.[26] In the pursuit of stimulation, they may also use alcohol and drugs, gamble, drive cars at high speeds, and seek sexual adventures. Frank Farley has identified what he calls a Type T (or "Big T") personality to describe such individuals.[27] The "T" stands for thrill seekers. The "Big T" personality anchors one end of a continuum; at the other end is the opposite "Little t" personality who avoids risks and unfamiliar places and people. Farley claims that these two personality types are relatively rare because most people have personalities that fall somewhere in between these two extremes. The "Big T" craves novelty and excitement, while the "Little t" desires routine and safe situations and activities.

Farley believes everyone seeks to maintain an optimal level of arousal (defined as feeling alert and "alive"). If arousal is too strong or too weak, people compensate by choosing experiences that are either stimulating or relaxing. "Big T" individuals need high levels of stimulation to achieve an optimal level of arousal because they were born, in Farley's view, with an unusually low capacity for arousal. So it takes higher than normal levels of stimulation for "Big Ts" to feel aroused and alive, and risk taking is how they reach these levels.

As a group, Farley observed, "Big Ts" tend to be more creative, extroverted, and risk oriented than other people. "Big Ts" were also significantly more likely to be males and young (16 to 24 years are the peak period for the expression of "Big T" personality traits—the same period when they peak physically). While the willingness to take risks associated with the "Big T" personality may be essential in achieving success in some situations, Farley points to the existence of a dark side, with some "Big Ts" going so far as to commit crimes for the sake of stimulation. His basic message, however, is that extreme thrill-seekers constitute a specific personality type: the "Big T."

Another thrill-seeking personality type is suggested by Marvin Zuckerman. This is the high-sensation seeking (HSS) personality.[28] Zuckerman explains that the HSS personality trait is associated with someone who has a tendency to seek varied, complex, and intense sensations and experiences, including a readiness to take risks for the sake of having such experiences. This trait is prevalent among individuals who are typically impulsive, highly social, and uninhibited. They have a strong aversion to low-sensation situations. They favor friends and spouses who are similar to them over those who do not have the HSS personality.

Zuckerman suggests that the brains of sensation seekers may be biochemically different from the brains of other people. The enzyme monoamine oxidase B (MAO B) is believed to have a major role in regulating arousal, inhibition, and pleasure. When Zuckerman tested HSS individuals, he observed unusually low MAO B levels. MAO B's specific function in the brain is to regulate at least three neurotransmitters: norepinephrine, which stimulates arousal; dopamine, which promotes the sensation of pleasure in response to arousal; and serotonin, which by repressing norepinephrine inhibits arousal. High-sensation seekers, Zuckerman suspects, have lower-base levels of norepinephrine and require more stimulation before serotonin is triggered. HSS individuals may also have lower levels of dopamine. Consequently, they may be in a chronic state of underarousal and need the higher levels of stimulation present in extreme risks in order to be rewarded by dopamine's pleasure reaction. Less risky activities do not satisfy them. Whether this is actually so, however, is not yet known, as Zuckerman's theory awaits proof. In any case, he does not claim that MAO B differences are the sole reason why people seek thrills and notes that brain chemistry may be only part of the answer. The individual's upbringing, experiences, class circumstances, and other factors could play central roles as well.

Zuckerman bases his research on a psychological scale he developed to measure sensation-seeking tendencies. Known as the Zuckerman Sensation Seeking Scale Form V (SSSV), the instrument contains four subscales: (1) Thrill and Adventure Seeking (TAS), measuring the desire to participate in risky, impulsive, and adventurous sports and activities; (2) Experience Seeking (ES), reflecting the desire to pursue new experiences and sensations; (3) Disinhibition (DIS), measuring impulsive, extroverted behavior; and (4) Boredom Susceptibility (BS), testing tolerance for boring and repetitive experiences. The four subscale scores are combined to produce a total score for sensation seeking. People who score high have been found to be attracted to extreme, high-risk sports, as well as to drug and alcohol use, cigarette smoking, high-risk sexual behavior, stimulating foods, and speeding.[29] Mountain climbers, skydivers, and motorcycle racers, and participants in similar sports all scored particularly high on the SSSV. Males also scored significantly higher than females.

A major difference between high- and low-sensation seekers may be that the highs are better able to quickly process sensory information—such as when they are snowboarding rapidly down a mountain. That is, their reflexes may be more oriented to the task ahead, allowing them to focus more quickly and adjust to the physical demands of their situation. They stay focused, when low-sensation seekers might panic in the same circumstances, freeze, or make a mistake. A genetic component to thrill-seeking may also be present, but if so, the gene has not been found.

Greg Soden, in his book *Falling*, suggests that the most efficient way to satisfy the needs of high-sensation seekers is the experience of falling through the air as occurs in skydiving and bungee jumping or the sustained, moment-to-moment risk of falling seen in rock climbing and mountaineering.[30] He says that activities exploiting the sensation of falling are the ultimate high. Jumping from an airplane and descending by parachute is such a high. One skydiver described his first jump this way:

> I was not afraid. I loved the ride. . . . The rawest amateur, in a cheapo "rag" chute, I felt like an eagle. I understood the power, the speed, the grace of flying. I was alone. The other parachutists were behind and higher than I was. I had the morning sky to myself.[31]

Parachutists also often feel a gush of satisfaction, pleasure, and well-being on landing unharmed. But the most thrilling part is exiting an aircraft in flight, experiencing free fall and opening the parachute, followed by the descent to ground with its visual and sensory experience of sail-like motion, sky, clouds, and the oncoming earth rising to catch the jumper. Soden explains that another type of thrill associated with falling is experiencing the risk that one may fall from a great height. Consequently, being on something towering above the ground, something that one can fall off, and traversing its surfaces can be exciting for high-sensation seekers. Soden reports that sports that can deliver this sensation, like mountain boarding (skateboards with small tires), skateboard jumping, and aerial surfing are constantly being invented. Amusement park rides cater to the falling sensation as well. Roller coasters, for example, are modified into loops, corkscrews, sharpened and lengthened descents, and the like, while new rides, like parachute and elevator drops, are featured too. The sensation of falling, Soden asserts, stirs up strong emotions, although he recognizes that not everyone is in agreement about its desirability. He states:

> Falling can feel like rapture, or if you're taken unwillingly, like rape. People violently disagree about avoiding its dangers and exploring its pleasures— even what those dangers and pleasures are. Free-soloist rock climbers—those who clamber up thousand-foot cliffs without ropes—will tell you that being on the knife-edge of the sensation makes them feel alive the way no other experience can. Critics—including some other climbers—say free soloists are simply insane.[32]

Edgeworkers

The sociological theory that best characterizes extreme sports participants is Stephen Lyng's theory of edgework.[33] As discussed in the first chapter, edgework refers to situations in which the skilled performance of a dangerous activity is the focus for the individual and others who witness the action. Edgework means skirting the edge between safety and danger, and "edgeworkers" are the people who engage in such pursuits. Lyng suggests that while most people seek to reduce threats to their well-being, others actively seek experiences with a high potential for personal injury or death. Risk taking is necessary for their well-being.

This is seen in the relatively new extreme sport of pond swooping that involves body-skimming across a pond at speeds up to 70 miles per hour. Participants parachute from an altitude of 5,000 feet using a small canopy that allows them to descend much faster than a larger parachute. When they reach 500 feet, they start spiraling to pick up speed in what looks like a free-fall death plunge—only to pull out by suddenly banking toward the pond, dipping one or two feet into the water, and skimming the surface to the far bank like a barefoot water-skier. The amount of control the participants have when they skim over the water determines how well their proficiency is rated in this sport that has an annual national competition. Pond swoopers are sometimes killed—especially when failing to come out of the plunge during their approach to the water. Nevertheless, this high-speed, high-performance parachuting attracts participants who are usually former sky divers desirous of moving on to something more exciting. Such persons often describe themselves as "speed freaks," since swooping is like doing a high dive with a parachute. In the words of one pond swooper:

> Yes, you have to dive to pick up speed, and if you mess it up, you're going to Die. . . . It's dangerous, but for some of us, [it's the] only time we're in control of our own destiny. If this sport was totally safe, most of these guys wouldn't be here.[34]

Pond swoopers and other edgeworkers share at least one common feature of their activities. According to Lyng, they all do things that involve a clear threat to their well-being and sense of an orderly existence. Perhaps they share another: they also try to exhibit skill at avoiding harm that they can claim as a special ability. "This unique skill," states Lyng, "which applies to all types of edgework, is the ability to maintain control over a situation that verges on complete chaos, a situation most people would regard as entirely uncontrollable."[35] Edgeworkers regard this skill as a special form of "mental toughness," which, in essence, is an innate survival capacity that allows them to respond instinctively to danger without having to think. When someone is injured or killed, edgeworkers often rationalize the person did not have enough innate survival capacity. Lyng also argues that the edgework experience involves alterations in perception and consciousness as it takes place. He says: "Participants in many different types of edgework report that, at the height of the experience (as they approach the edge), their perceptual field becomes highly focused: background factors recede from view, and their perception narrows to only those factors that immediately determine success or failure in negotiating the edge."[36]

Success at edgework understandably promotes feelings of omnipotence, exhilaration, and exaggerated prowess for the edgeworker and his or her fellow edgeworkers. There is a tendency to believe they are a "special breed" possessing unique death-dying skills; hence, they constitute an elite.

Lyng finds that much of the motivation to engage in edgework is in the desire for creative, skillful, and self-determining action that many people, both blue-collar workers and professionals, lack in their jobs. That many edgeworkers have somewhat mundane and ordinary day-to-day jobs and that their edgework is an escape from their work, underscores the importance of edgework in their lives. However, it is not just the thrill of the risks they undertake or a desire to gamble with danger that is their goal. Rather, it is the chance to use their skill in overcoming a challenge. What they risk is their personal competence, and what they win by engaging in successful edgework is self-confirmation of that competence.

Factors Influencing Participation

The finding that extreme sports participants have "extreme" (wild and crazy) personalities is hardly a surprise, given the great enthusiasm they have for their death- and injury-defying activities and the thrilling sensations they and those who witness them experience when their stunts are performed. Still, individuality and personalities are not the complete explanation for participation in extreme sports. Participants perform their actions in groups that encourage, admire, and cheer on one another. There is an audience for what they do, congratulations from others for their successes, and remorse for their failures—especially those that result in death or serious injury. Consequently, group influence and recognition is a major factor in stimulating participation in extreme sports.

It also seems highly likely that social-class position joins a thrill-seeking personality and group influence to play the key roles in fostering extreme sports participation. The poor, lacking the necessary social and financial capital, are, as indicated, generally excluded from such sports. Risk taking, in the context of extreme sports, is a middle-class endeavor, though some individuals from the working class edge their way in. French sociologist Pierre Bourdieu helps us to understand this outcome with his notion of the "distance from necessity."[37] He points out that the more distant a person is from foraging for economic necessities like food and shelter, the greater the freedom and time that individual has to develop and refine personal tastes in line with a more privileged class status. People in the lower class, in turn, tend to adopt the tastes consistent with their class position, in which acquiring items of necessity is paramount. With certain traditional sports like sailing, downhill and cross-country skiing, golf, tennis, and horseback riding, Bourdieu observes that the less affluent, including members of the working class, not only face economic barriers to participation, but the hidden entry requirements of family tradition, early training, obligatory dress and behavior, and socialization. While extreme sports do not have the refinement or family traditions of these conventional sports, they nonetheless require time, money, and their own form of socialization.

The development of the extreme sport of bungee jumping provides an example. Bungee jumping originated in the Vanuatu Islands of the South Pacific, where natives engaged in "land diving," or jumping from 100-foot towers headfirst toward the ground. The point of contact on the ground was a soft, mound of soil, but the most important measure for the divers was attaching vines to their ankles to break their fall. As Soden suggests, the sport had its genesis among the natives when a man chased his wife to the top of a palm tree when he discovered she had taken a lover.[38] The wife tied a vine to her leg and jumped off the tree when her husband lunged at her. She lived but he died after falling to the ground.

According to the local legend, the men decided it would be a good idea to practice the stunt in case they found themselves in the same predicament. So they began land diving and forbade women from participating. The idea was not only to demonstrate male superiority, but also to impress the women by defying death, as the community gathered to watch the jumping performances. Eventually, a Western journalist in his twenties visited the islands for *National Geographic* and insisted on trying the sport himself. His account was published in 1970.

In 1977, a small group of young, affluent British men met on a mountain in Switzerland, where they had gathered for hang-gliding. They re-

tired later to a local pub where they discovered that they had much in common. Soden writes:

> All of them had a craving for excitement and hadn't found much of it in traditional sport, which is why they had been attracted to hang gliding. Something must be done, they agreed. Existing sports had to be pushed to new limits, and even better—new sports that delivered a bigger kick had to be invented. They would be a club—the Dangerous Sports Club, one of them dubbed it, a name that was satirical on the face of it because they were hardly organized enough to be a club, and much they would do would have nothing to do with danger or sports, unless you consider drinking a risky athletic event.[39]

For the next few years they met annually, mainly as an excuse for heavy drinking, and doing something bizarre like having a party atop a stone slab in the Atlantic Ocean, several miles off the coast of Scotland and jumping into the sea 70 feet below, ski races in Switzerland carried out in a bath tub, a rowboat, a toilet, and even a grand piano played by a drunken member as it slid down a mountain. They also did whitewater kayaking, and later hang-gliding off Mount Kilimanjaro in Africa. But they had not invented anything. That changed when one of their members, looking at a suspension bridge in England remembered the land-diving article in *National Geographic* and came up with the idea of jumping off the bridge using bungee cords instead of vines. He thought the cords would hold a man's weight. "At least that was the theory," states Soden.[40] And a theory was all they would have as they decided it would not be sporting to test the idea in advance.

Deciding to jump on April Fools' Day in 1979, they threw a wild all-night party the night of March 31st for themselves and their friends. The next day, when the police called to the scene had left, thinking the jump was a hoax, four club members, dressed in top hats and tuxedos, one carrying a bottle of champagne, put on their equipment and jumped off the bridge. The first jumper:

> . . . fell like a stone, and his formal attire looked like an undertaker perhaps arranging for his own funeral. More than a hundred feet below them, he practically vanished against the dark river. Then, halfway to his doom, the cord ran our of slack and began to stretch. He slowed—and then began to rise. It was working.[41]

The others then jumped, the police returned to arrest them for disturbing the peace, and they were all suddenly famous since a newspaper photographer and film camera crew were there. The publicity was enormous, and the Dangerous Sports Club became the darling of the British press. For their next event, members eluded the police to bungee jump off

San Francisco's Golden Gate Bridge, where in the water below a boat waited to pick them up. Shown on television, this event made bungee jumping known to millions of people. "Although the Dangerous Sports Club had managed to invent only one new sport," states Soden, "it was a sport that delivered an unparalleled visceral kick—a kick that would prove to be a siren call for a significant portion of the population."[42] For some people, extreme sports and the thrills associated with them are indeed a siren call.

Consequently, extreme sports require not only a thrill-seeking personality and a group to nurture and approve of the experience, but also the time and money that comes with being a member of an affluent social strata.

Conclusion

The risk voluntarily undertaken in extreme sports at some point falls on the individual risk-taker. This point comes when the risk-taker moves to the edge between safety and security and initiates edgework. Risk taking in such events is not a team sport, but an individual skill performance since only one person is on stage or on exhibit during the moment of risk. However, extreme sports belong inherently to the sociological domain in that they involve audiences, social support from groups, particular modes of dress and equipment, and membership in a social class that provides the financial and temporal freedom to engage in them.

Returning again to the model of risk-taking behavior shown in Figure 1-1 (in Chapter 1), it is clear that extreme sports participants are at the high end of the risk-response continuum. Their location in this continuum is that of *"active seeking,"* with the bungee jumper the typical example of people in this group. This category of risk-takers has high agency (choice) in that they are all willing volunteers. In addition, the social structural conditions of their lives supply the resources that enable them to carry out their risky choices. They are far from being passive victims of risk behavior. Rather, extreme sports participants have such high control over their risk response that they are the ultimate risk-takers who delight in a skilled performance. They actively seek out risks that put them precisely at the edge of harm. The closer they get to that edge, and survive it, the better they feel about themselves and the experience.

Notes

1. Catherine Palmer. 2002. "'Shit Happens': The Selling of Risk in Extreme Sport." *Australian Journal of Anthropology*, 13: 323–336.
2. Trisha Blackmar and Mark Beech. 2003. "Their Time Is Now: Bigger Waves, Bigger Air, Whiter Water: Meet Three Teens Who Are Redefining the Shredding Edge of Their Sports." *Sports Illustrated*, 99 (July 7): A12.
3. Devin Gordon and Gegax T. Trent. 2002. "Going Extreme." *Newsweek*, 139 (February 25): 48.
4. Roger Rosenblatt. 1999. "'The Whole World Is Jumpable': The Most Extreme Sport of All Often Kills Its Players. What is its strange appeal?" *Time*, 154 (July 19): 94.
5. Gregg Bennett and Robin K. Henson. 2003. "Perceived Status of the Action Sports Segment Among College Students." *International Sports Journal*, 7: 124–138.
6. Ibid.
7. Joan Raymond. 2002."Going to Extremes." *American Demographics*, 24 (June): 28–30.
8. Austin Murphy. 2003. "Higher, Faster, Louder." *Sports Illustrated*, 98 (February 17): A16.
9. Rebecca Heath. 1997. "You Can Buy a Thrill: Chasing the Ultimate Rush." *American Demographics*, 19: 47–51.
10. Ibid.
11. Matthew Klein. 1998. "Power-Trippers: Hard Adventure Travel Gets Blood Pumping and Dollars Flowing." *American Demographics*, 20: 1213.
12. Palmer, p. 324.
13. Ibid., p. 328.
14. Jon Krakauer. 1997. *Into Thin Air*. New York: Villard.
15. Ibid., p. 7.
16. Ibid., p. 1.
17. Ibid., p. 6.
18. Ibid., p. 9.
19. Ibid., p. 275.
20. John Derbyshire. 2000. "The Eclipse of Risk." *National Review*, 52 (October 23): 67.
21. Kristin L. Anderson. 1999. "Snowboarding: The Construction of Gender in an Emerging Sport." *Journal of Sport and Social Issues*, 23: 55–79.

22. Joanne Kay. 1998. "Extreme Sport, Gender, and Risk." Paper presented to the International Sociological Association World Congress of Sociology meeting, Montreal, July.
23. Ibid.
24. Brendan I. Koerner. 1997. "Extreeeme." *U.S. News and World Report*, 122 (June 30): 50.
25. Paul Bellaby and David Lawrenson. 2001. "Approaches to the Risk of Riding Motorcycles: Reflections on the Problem of Reconciling Statistical Risk Assessment and Motorcyclists Own Reasons for Riding." *Sociological Review*, 49: 368–388. Thomas E. Risk. 1999. "The Wild New West." *Atlantic Monthly*, 283 (June): 50-54.
26. William Pickett, Michael J. Garner, William F. Boyce, and Matthew A. King. 2002. "Gradients in Risk for Youth Injury Associated with Multiple-Risk Behaviours: A Study of 11,329 Canadian Adolescents." *Social Science and Medicine*, 55: 1055–1065.
27. Frank Farley. 1989. "Taking Risks and Seeking Stimulation: The Type T Personality." *Psychology Today*, 118: 60–62.
28. Marvin Zuckerman. 1994. *Behavioral Expressions and Biosocial Bases of Sensation Seeking.* Cambridge, UK: Cambridge University Press.
29. Marjorie J. Malkin and Erik R Rabinowitz. 1998. *Parks and Recreation*, 33: 34–40.
30. Garrett Soden. 2003. *Falling.* New York: Norton.
31. Thomas Fensch. 1980. *Skydiving Book.* Mountain View, CA: Anderson World.
32. Soden, pp. 15–16.
33. Stephen Lyng. 1990. "Edgework: A Social Psychological Analysis of Voluntary Risk Taking." *American Journal of Sociology*, 85: 851–886.
34. Corey Kilgannon. 2004. "New Thrill for the Bored-With-Just Parachuting Set." *New York Times* (August 23): A21.
35. Lyng, p. 859.
36. Ibid., p. 861.
37. Pierre Bourdieu. 1984. *Distinction.* Cambridge, MA: Harvard University Press.
38. Soden, p. 2.
39. Ibid., pp. 5–6.
40. Ibid., p. 7.
41. Ibid., p. 8.
42. Ibid., p. 11.

Why People Take Risks

In the first chapter we learned that in contemporary society risk signifies danger, threat, or harm—something potentially bad. Some risks are associated with health, and why people take these particular risks is the focus of this book. The evidence explaining unsafe sexual practices, alcohol abuse, illicit drug use, smoking, and participation in extreme sports has been reviewed to answer why, if these activities can harm or even kill, do people undertake them? The best overall answer is that apparently they do so for reasons of pleasure-seeking and its close companion, thrill-seeking.

This conclusion goes against much of the literature in the social sciences that represents risk taking as the "product of ignorance or irrationality."[1] Thus, most accounts of risk taking depict it as something to be avoided, not embraced. In the first chapter, for example, we saw how leading sociologists like Ulrich Beck[2] and Anthony Giddens[3] described the "risk society" in which institutions and business corporations inherently produce risks associated with desired goods, products, and activities that become a cause for public worry and concern. "Risk society" theorists, as Deborah Lupton observes, focus their analysis on macrostructural factors originating in society at-large and producing risks that cause concern among the general public.[4] They argue that risks produced in late-modern societies have increased, become globalized, and are more difficult to avoid than in past eras. Examples of such risks are the deaths and injuries caused by automobiles, which at the same time vastly improve transportation, and the adverse health conditions caused by environmental pollution resulting from the manufacture of desired industrial products.

Risk society theories are essentially theories of risk avoidance. Risk avoidance is seen as a general orientation of people and governments in the risk society when it comes to both personal behavior and public policy. Therefore, as Lupton and John Tulloch point out, risk avoidance is typically depicted in the social science literature as rational behavior, while risk taking is viewed as irrational or stemming from ignorance of the possible consequences.[5] The idea that risk taking could also be intentional and rational is either not considered or dismissed as foolhardy. "So, too," state Lupton and Tulloch, "in the sociological literature dominated by the writings of Beck and Giddens, the human actor is portrayed as anxious and fearful of risk, eager to acquire knowledge as to best avoid becoming a victim of risk."[6]

However, as shown throughout this book, while some people are indeed victims of their own risk taking, others deliberately choose to undertake risks and find the experience not only pleasurable, but perhaps self-fulfilling and a validation of their self-worth. As Lupton and Tulloch conclude, risk taking is more complex than traditional social science literature suggests and far from being either an unknowing and unavoidable activity. Some people knowingly seek out risks, and the only sociological theory that has focused on such individuals is Stephen Lyng's theory of edgework.[7] His introduction of the term *edgeworkers*—people who deliberately skirt the edge between safety and danger in their activities—accurately describes individuals who participate in extreme sports, but it does not account for those people who voluntarily take risks because it's their job or lack the capacity to do otherwise. A more expansive model of risk taking is shown in Figure 1-1 (in Chapter 1) and repeated in this chapter in Figure 7-1. Before reviewing this model, we will look at the motivation behind risk taking.

Feeling Good

The accounts of risk taking in this book show that people risk their health because it makes them *feel good*. They do these things even though the state of addiction inherent in chronic heavy drinking, illicit drug use, and smoking causes them to feel very bad when the addictive substance is not readily available. Damage from these substances to the liver, central nervous system, lungs, heart, and other parts of the body is also discomforting and potentially fatal. The thrill associated with a skillful performance in an extreme sport can be replaced by excruciating pain from a serious injury due to participation in that sport. And even sex, which is one of the most pleasurable human experiences—perhaps the most pleasurable for many people—can weaken the body's immune system and cause death if it results in the transmission of HIV/AIDS. Nonetheless, people still take the risks and, predictably, many of them die as a result.

While these modes of risk taking may be dismissed by some people as irrational, foolhardy, and ignorant, it is clear from the accounts presented in this book that often the behavior is very rational and calculated by the risk-taker to achieve a desired end state. Risk taking is clearly a different form of social behavior than the risk-avoidance discussed by Beck and Giddens. Of course, pleasure-seeking and thrill-seeking are far from being the sole explanations for risk taking. Some people have personalities that attract them to risky situations, although more than personality—specifically, the social environment—is typically involved in risk-taking decisions. Risk taking is nurtured and stimulated through social interaction with other people. In fact, accounts in this book show that the first step in risk taking is learning how to do it from someone else. The learning experience includes the experienced risk-taker guiding and interpreting what the experience signifies for the novice. Risk taking does not begin in isolation from other people, but is initiated in concert with them. Some people take risks because it is their job (e.g., combat infantryman, firefighter, and police officer), while others are simply subject to risk (e.g., sex workers). However, in all these situations, risk taking is carried out in relation to other individuals.

Many people appear to be attracted to the pleasures or thrills associated with risks that adversely affect health. Smoking, for example, causes the deaths of some 440,000 people annually in the United States. When smoking-related mortality from around the world is tabulated, the number of deaths ranges in the millions every year. Simply knowing the potential risk of death contained in a tobacco product does not necessarily prevent smoking. It is a common refrain for smokers to say they know they should not smoke and smoke anyway.

This situation makes the pursuit of pleasure seem almost thoughtless, in that it occurs regardless of personal awareness of the potential risk. Many years ago the Austrian psychoanalyst Sigmund Freud (1856–1939) argued that part of the human personality, which he called the id, is oriented toward finding pleasure (avoiding pain and seeking pleasure) through activities like eating certain foods and having sex.[8] Instincts, in his view, provide the energy that operates the personality. He argued that human behavior is driven by powerful instinctual forces that the individual not only is unable to control, but in fact is unaware of their existence. The personality itself has three components: the id, ego, and superego. The id seeks instinctual gratification by following the pleasure principle of reflex action. Guided by the primary process that produces a memory image of the object needed to reduce instinctual tension, the id leads the personality in that direction to find fulfillment.

Freud considered the id to be a particularly strong force in driving the personality toward pleasurable objects. The failure of the id to easily find satisfaction energizes the ego consisting of memory, judgment, perception, and reason. Guided by the reality principle, the ego searches the environment for the object needed to satisfy the id or find an acceptable solution to the id's need. The superego is the moral or judicial branch of the personality, with the power to reward (through pride) or punish (through feelings of inferiority or guilt by way of the conscience). The superego drives the personality to seek what is ideal, and its aim is to achieve perfection. In its basic form, Freud's concept of the personality is a system of psychic energy consisting of the id striving for pleasure in order to satisfy fundamental instincts, the superego striving for perfection, and the ego balancing the two drives with a sense of reality. Freud theorizes that if the ego is weak and the id or superego too strong, then the individual will have a maladjusted personality.

This model portrays people in general as being propelled by their instincts into situations in which their goal is to find pleasure. They appear to be almost robotic as they are mindlessly driven by their instincts toward gaining the pleasure they desire. Applied to risk taking, this perspective projects the image of risk-takers as dominated by their id. They unthinkingly disregard the negative consequences of what they desire in return for the immediate rush of pleasure. People thus do risky things simply because it makes them feel good or thrills them. While this view might seem to account for the actions of some risk-takers, we have no evidence that the id, ego, and superego actually exist. Freud's theory also overlooks cognitive development (e.g., learning and the role of education) in influencing behavior, and there are several other criticisms not central to this discussion—including the overemphasis on childhood experiences reasserting themselves as psychological problems in adult behavior. These criticisms have significantly lessened Freud's influence in psychiatry and the behavioral sciences. Moreover, regarding the focus of this book, his theory of the personality also overlooks the capability of people to engage in reflexive thinking, an ability that makes possible the control and organization of a person's behavior in relation to his or her social circumstances. This book argues that a person's social circumstances and control of his or her conduct have a great deal to do with risk taking.

For example, in sociology we know from symbolic interaction theory that human beings have the capacity to think and decide on their own or with other people how to act in particular social situations. George Herbert Mead, in his most-influential book *Mind, Self, and Society*, rejected the idea that people are robots responding automatically to their instincts.[9] Rather, people react to instincts and other stimuli according to their perceptions and definitions of the situations in which they find themselves. In terms of behavior, people can choose which stimuli they wish to respond to or even be creative and do something different. They make the decisions that guide the manner, form, and style of their interaction with other people. The key factor is the definition or perception of the situation by those involved. This is not to say that people are uninfluenced by social conditions over which they have no control, such as losing one's job in an economic downturn. Symbolic interaction theory suggests that people cope with the reality of their circumstances based on their understanding of the situation. The usefulness of symbolic interaction theory to our understanding of risk taking lies in its helping us see that such behavior is based on a person's interpretation of the situation and is a deliberate social act by the individual that can be either active or passive—depending on the social circumstances.

Yet it should not be presumed that symbolic interaction theory depicts the individual as making behavioral choices in a social vacuum without considering the views of other people or that of the group as a whole to which he or she belongs. Mead states that if someone is to develop socially in the fullest sense, that person must be aware of the attitudes and perceptions of other people regarding the same social activity in which he or she is engaged. He also suggests that groups have their own norms, values, goals, and views that influence the individual's perspective in the form of a "generalized other." The term *generalized other* refers to the organized attitudes of groups and communities as they enter into the thinking of the individual. Society itself would not be possible, according to Mead, unless the individuals belonging to it are able to take the general attitudes of others involved in the same complex, cooperative group activities and direct their behavior in accordance with the group's perspective. States Mead:

> It is in this form of the generalized other that the social process influences the behavior of the individuals involved in it and carrying it on, that is, that the community exercises control over the conduct of its individual members; for it is in this form that the social process or community enters as a determining factor into the individual's thinking.[10]

Mead therefore recognized the potential for larger social forces to influence microlevel forms of social interaction between people—even though his focus is on how individuals construct their own social reality. Sociological concepts reflecting literally all theories of social life attest to the fact that something (structure) exists beyond the individual to give rise to customary patterns of behavior. These concepts range from Mead's view of the generalized other as the organized attitudes of the whole community and the social process through which "the community exercises control over the conduct of its members"[11] to Emile Durkheim's notion of social facts as "every way of acting, fixed or not, capable of exercising on the individual an external constraint."[12] Consequently, risk taking as a form of social behavior involves the interaction of both agency (choosing) and structure (empowerment or constraint).

Model of Risk Taking

To summarize the view of risk taking featured in this book, we return once again to the model first presented in Chapter 1, and as indicated, repeated here in Figure 7-1. This figure shows that the types of risk response are strongly influenced by the twin processes of agency and structure. Agency is the process in which individuals, influenced by their past but also oriented toward the future (as a capacity to imagine alternative possibilities) and the present (as a capacity to consider both past habits and future situations within the contingencies of the moment), critically evaluate and choose their course of action.[13] While risk-taking situations involve choices, whatever choices are made are strongly affected by structure. Structure refers to rules (and norms) and resources (especially those associated with social class position) that enable or make possible those choices, or

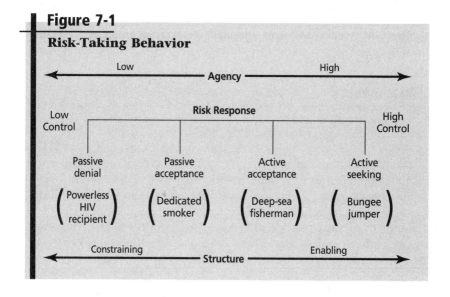

Figure 7-1

Risk-Taking Behavior

constrains and possibly prevents potential choices from being realized.[14] The enabling function refers to the use of resources to increase the range and style of options an actor can choose from, but constraint means that resources invariably limit choices about what is possible. As Zygmunt Bauman observes, individual choices in *all* circumstances are confined by two sets of constraints: (1) choosing from among what is available, and (2) social rules or codes telling the individual the rank order and appropriateness of preferences.[15]

Although it has been argued that agency can never be completely determined by structure, it is also clear that there is no circumstance in which agency actually becomes "free" of structure.[16] Choices are always affected in some way by structure that either empowers or limits them. Therefore, while agency refers to the capacity to choose behavior, structure pertains to regularities in social interaction (e.g., institutions, roles), systematic social relationships (e.g., group affiliations, class, and other forms of social stratification), and resources that influence the person to go in particular directions rather than in other directions that might be taken. While structure operates to constrain health risk taking by limiting the availability of alcohol, cigarettes, and drugs to people without the financial resources to obtain them in abundance or to constrain people subject to strong group norms rejecting such use, it enables those with the resources and social support to acquire them. Another example is participation in extreme sports. Although many people regard such participation as foolhardy, others—for whom such sports are exciting—admire and appreciate the daring performances, and participants feel good about themselves because of it. As one former rodeo rider says:

> I'm thinking probably the most focused risk-taking, where you really can't predict what might be the outcome of the activity at all, is riding in a rodeo, which I did over about a two-year period, and each experience is unique and absolutely unpredictable. What it is that you get from success is a degree of personal satisfaction and self-esteem as a result of taking, accepting a risk and being successful. And if you said to me, you know, "Is it worth it?", I'd have to say "Yes!".[17]

Agency and structure therefore flank the risk-response continuum shown in Figure 7-1. When agency is high and structure is enabling, people have high control over their risk response; conversely, when agency is low and structure is most constraining, they lack control over risk taking. Therefore, as depicted in Figure 7-1, people at the lowest end of the risk-response continuum are in passive denial (e.g., the powerless HIV-recipient). They are passive in responding to risk because there is nothing they can do about it. They are constrained by structure because they are dependent on others for financial and social support, and have a low capacity for exercising agency in a risky situation. Their typical coping strategy is denial in that they tend to deny the risk exists or that they will be the ones to be harmed. Fate or luck, not themselves, will decide the outcome, and they let the situation run as "fate" would have it. An example of this type of risk-taker appears in an account of HIV-infected women in northern Virginia:

> "We come from a culture where we just do sex, we don't talk about it," said [a female] coordinator of the AIDS outreach program of the Urban League of Hampton Roads. The vast majority of the infected mothers are black. "We don't ask our black men, 'Have you ever had sex with another man? Have you ever exchanged sex for drugs or money?'" Women who are economically dependent on men aren't likely to make an issue of it, even if they know the risks.[18]

Next on the risk-response continuum are people in passive acceptance (e.g., the dedicated smoker). They could exercise agency and quit smoking, for example, but do not despite their awareness of the risk. The structure of their lives operates to constrain change. They may socialize mostly with smokers, since spouses and family members smoke, friends smoke, co-workers smoke, and their social class (lower or working class) does not necessarily view smoking as deviant behavior. One man in London, for example, has recently argued that it should not become the first city in Great Britain to ban smoking in public places, including pubs, as happened in Ireland. He says medical experts need to "get real." He puts it this way:

> The whole of the medical world might say smoking is a killer. Yes, it's like life itself, a slow killer. . . . You can no more stop people smoking than stop the waves. If it knocks some time off your life, it's only time at the end of it. So what?[19]

Some smokers in the passive-acceptance category go so far as to view cigarettes as their friend, seeing them as a source of comfort and companionship. According to one study, heavy smokers (people who smoke 25 or more cigarettes a day) know they should not smoke, but get angry that this source of physical pleasure might be taken from them.[20] The study concludes:

> Over 90% believed that even though smoking was dangerous, it was their "friend." The danger of losing a friend was more threatening to them than the dangers of smoking, and they worried about what would take the place of cigarettes emotionally.[21]

The next highest in the risk-response continuum are people in active acceptance (e.g., deep-sea fishermen). These are individuals whose jobs place them in risk-taking situations. Soldiers fighting in wartime, police officers who risk their lives in apprehending criminals, and sex workers routinely exposed to sexually-transmitted diseases are other examples of active acceptance. Risk taking is something they are paid to accept. They have the capacity to exercise agency and are enabled by the structure surrounding their occupation to deal with risky situations. As one indoor sex worker described her support system in dealing with a violent client: "We have CS gas here and everything and I wouldn't be afraid to use it. We have an alert buzzer and in the bedroom we have a pickaxe handle."[22]

But sometimes safety measures fail. If deep-sea fishing is the most dangerous of all civilian occupations, it is especially so during winter months or during storms at any time of year. In Alaska, during the winter, ice can collect on the pilothouse of a fishing boat, shifting the boat's center of gravity and causing it to capsize. Crews will attack the ice with crowbars and baseball bats in what can amount to a fight for survival. Waves and high winds can dislodge equipment on the deck and knock someone overboard. A person falling into the water can freeze to death in about the time it takes a cup of coffee to cool. Alaskan fishermen have the most lethal job in the country. Whereas the accidental death rate for all U.S. occupations is about 7 per 100,000 workers annually, Alaskan fishermen have a death rate of 200 per 100,000. For crab fishermen in Alaskan waters, the rate is even higher, around 660 deaths per 100,000 in some years. Says [one crab fisherman]: "Basically, you've got to watch your ass all the time. You've got to be really alert to what's around you. But fatigue can get to people."[23]

Despite the risks and the hard work, fishing boats still return to the sea. One man, who fished for crab on the Bering Sea off Alaska for four years, told a reporter for the *Anchorage Daily News* that he escaped with no serious injuries, worked harder than he ever had, and enjoyed the financial fortune that came with a good fishing season. He felt positive about meeting the personal challenges the work demanded. Nevertheless, it was dangerous work. He recollected:

> . . . the danger was driven home to me in 2001, during the February (snow crab) season. I was a deckhand on the 155-foot F/V Centarus, a 600-ton boat that was one of the fleet's largest.
>
> We were more than 100 miles out to sea, riding out a storm that had come up the night before. Our captain had throttled down the engines so we were going about 2 knots, just enough to keep us pointed into the oncoming waves. The boat plowed into the waves, riding up the crests, pausing, then plunging down into the troughs.
>
> Late in the morning there was an especially long pause at the top of one of those waves, followed by an especially long drop into the trough. We slammed into the face of an immense rouge wave, and the entire boat was submerged for a moment.
>
> The impact blew out nine of the wheelhouse windows and crumpled the upper part of the steel wheelhouse. Several thousand gallons of frigid sea-water

poured into the boat. Our electronic navigational equipment was instantly destroyed, along with our heaters and radio equipment. Steering components were damaged, rendering us unable to control the rudders. The impact had also slightly bent the hull of the boat, although the damage was underneath and we did not learn of it until later.

It was winter in the Bering Sea, water was knee-deep in the galley, our lights were shorted out, we had no working radios and we were drifting. However, through some miracle, nobody was seriously injured.[24]

The crew pumped out the water and worked on repairing the steering. The captain activated the Emergency Position Indicating Radio Beacon that brought a Coast Guard search and rescue plane. The plane, in turn, radioed other boats that came to help. It took two days, but the steering was repaired enough to control the boat and the broken windows were covered with plywood. The ship and its crew resumed fishing and completed the season with the rest of the fleet. To turn back to port for repairs would have meant missing the season and facing a burden of unpaid debts if they returned empty-handed.

Highest on the risk continuum are people whose high level of agency and enabling structure provide time and financial resources that allow them to actively seek risk-taking situations (e.g., bungee jumping) and then to welcome them with enthusiasm. Risk avoidance is not a serious option. Risk taking is the optimal state of being and the thrill of being on the edge of safety and danger is a major focus of their lives. An example of these edgeworkers and the type of activities they are drawn to is shown in a newspaper story about Britain's top-ranked female skier in 2004. In it she says:

Between the ages of 11 and 19 I used to fly out to New Zealand and Australia every summer holiday on the last day of term for their winter and come back the day before school started again. New Zealand is so beautiful. Queenstown is a great ski resort . . . , but there's also so much else to do. You can ski in the morning and go bungee jumping or sky diving in the afternoon.[25]

During the spring months, according to the article, she goes scuba diving. On her first outing she traveled to Belize, was "wolf-whistled" by some U.S. Navy Seals, got to chatting with them, and ended up joining them for scuba diving: "I went straight in at the deep end: my first qualified dive was to 140 ft. I love sharks so I dived the Blue Hole and the diving was awesome."[26]

Competitive skiing, bungee jumping, sky diving, and scuba diving with sharks clearly qualifies someone who performs all (or one) of these activities to reside at the upper end of the risk-taking continuum. Such a person is obviously an active seeker of risks and thus serves to anchor the highest end of the continuum.

Conclusion

Although much of the work in sociology on risk has focused on risk avoidance, it is clear from the research that some people actively choose to be risk-takers and so deliberately place themselves in risky situations. Others cannot avoid being risk-takers because they are relatively powerless to do anything else. But either way, risk taking is a social activity. As Teela Sanders suggests, risk is not only an objective, calculable event associated with certain activities, but is linked to the individual and his or her social circumstances.[27] Risk-taking behavior in her view, and that of other scholars, including the author, "needs to be understood as a socially organized phenomenon rather than conceptualized only from the viewpoint of individual rationality."[28] Individuals cope with risks within the social context of their lives, including the organized relationships they have with other people.

With the exception of those whose risk taking is forced on them by others, the risk-taking experience and the dangers associated with it are largely undertaken for the pleasure of feeling good. This is apparently true for health risks ranging from unsafe sex and smoking to extreme sports. Even people who actively accept risks as part of their job tend to feel good about themselves for having mastered such risks.[29] Sometimes the simplest answers are best and that seems to be the case here: people risk their health primarily because they want to *feel good*.

Notes

1. Deborah Lupton and John Tulloch. 2002. "'Life Would Be Pretty Dull Without Risk': Voluntary Risk-Taking and Its Pleasure." *Health, Risk and Society*, 4: 113.
2. Ulrich Beck. 1992. *Risk Society: Towards a New Modernity*. Translated by Mark Ritter. London: Sage.
3. Anthony Giddens. 2000. *Runaway World*. New York: Routledge.
4. Deborah Lupton. 1999. "Introduction: Risk and Sociocultural Theory." In Deborah Lupton (ed.), *Risk and Sociocultural Theory*. Cambridge, UK: Cambridge University Press.
5. Lupton and Tulloch.

6. Ibid., p. 114.

7. Stephen Lyng. 1990. "Edgework: A Social Psychological Theory of Voluntary Risk Taking." *American Journal of Sociology*, 95: 851–886.

8. Sigmund Freud. 1953–1966. *Standard Edition of the Complete Psychological Works of Sigmund Freud*. London: Hogarth Press.

9. George Herbert Mead. 1934. *Mind, Self, and Society*. Chicago: University of Chicago Press.

10. George Herbert Mead. 1956. *On Social Psychology*, edited by Anselm Strauss. Chicago: University of Chicago Press.

11. Mead, *Mind, Self, and Society*, p. 155.

12. Emile Durkheim. 1950. *The Rules of Sociological Method*. New York: Free Press, p. 13.

13. Mustafa Emirbayer and Ann Mische. 1998. "What Is Agency?" *American Journal of Sociology*, 103: 962–1023.

14. William H. Sewell. 1992. "A Theory of Structure: Duality, Agency, and Transformation." *American Journal of Sociology*, 98: 1–29.

15. Zygmunt Bauman. 1999. *In Search of Politics*. Stanford, CA: Stanford University Press.

16. Emirbayer and Mische.

17. Lupton and Tulloch, p. 118.

18. Marie Joyce. 1995. "HIV Rises Sharply for Young Women in the Region. Chesapeake Has the State's Highest HIV Rate for Young Women." *Virginian* (May 26): A1.

19. Andr Paine. 2004. "David Hockney Stands Up for the Art of Smoking." *Evening Standard* (June 1): 3.

20. *Biotech Week*. 2004. "University of Washington: Heavy Smokers See Cigarettes as 'Friends.'" (Feb. 4): 557.

21. Ibid.

22. Teela Sanders. 2004. "A Continuum of Risk? The Management of Health, Physical and Emotional Risks by Female Sex Workers." *Sociology of Health and Illness*, 26: 557–574.

23. Bill Saporito. 1993. "The Most Dangerous Job in America." *Fortune* (May 31): 130.

24. Cade Smith. 2004. "Frontier Finale: With the End of Derby-Style Fisheries, Another Piece of Alaska Mythology Drifts into History. *Anchorage Daily News* (Oct. 25): D1.

25. Carl Wilkinson. 2004. "Escape: Tales from My Travels: Chemmy Alcott: 'I Never Get Sick of Seeing Snow: Britain's Top Female Skier Likes Scuba Diving When She's Not on the Slopes." *The Observer* (Oct. 3): 13.

26. Ibid.

27. Sanders, p. 558.

28. Ibid.

29. Smith.

Index